Managing
Web-Based Training

Learning Technologies

Managing
Web-Based Training

How to Keep Your Program on Track
and Make It Successful

Alan L. Ellis,
Ellen D. Wagner, and
Warren R. Longmire

Linking People,
Learning & Performance

Ordering information: Books published by the American Society for Training & Development can be ordered by calling 800.628.2783 or 703.683.8100.

Library of Congress Catalog Card Number: 99-72434
ISBN: 1-56286-115-8

Editor's note: We have done our level best to provide accurate URL addresses in this book. However, due to the ever-changing nature of the Web, some of these addresses may change.

Table of Contents

Managing the Development and Design of Web-Based Training

Evaluation and Maintenance Issues

About the Learning Technologies Series

For centuries, the technology for transferring skills and knowledge changed little—one human being taught others. Generations of classroom trainers deployed this time-honored "chalk-and-talk" approach. Only the advent of the film, the filmstrip, video, and the slide and overhead projectors marred an education landscape otherwise devoid of technological innovation. All of this, however, is currently undergoing rapid change—the snail-paced rate of innovation has given way to a torrent of change as new technologies create the possibility of more effective and efficient learning.

Increasingly, the transfer of information, knowledge, and skills can be facilitated by a variety of electronic media, often reducing the need for time-intensive transfer based on the interaction of human beings. This change represents both a challenge and an opportunity for professionals who specialize in workplace learning and performance.[1]

Managing Web-Based Training: How to Keep Your Program on Track and Make It Successful is the second book in a series of short, easily understood learning technologies books that will give these same professionals the tools to become part of this exciting technology revolution. Some books in this series will provide detailed step-by-step instructions on how to design and deliver Web-based instruction, and others in the series may examine how to evaluate the effectiveness of such training.

In addition to providing valuable information, these books will strive toward a consistent use of terminology to help standardize an increasingly confusing lexicon of terms. (See the Glossary for more on definitions associated with learning technologies.)

We hope this series of books will enable all learning and performance professionals to use these powerful new tools effectively.

---

[1]From November 1997 *Training & Development* magazine article, "Trends That Affect Learning and Performance Improvement" by ASTD Research staff: Laurie J. Bassi, Scott Cheney, and Mark Van Buren.

Preface

The World Wide Web and Web-based technologies have dramatically changed how training is delivered in corporations, government agencies, educational institutions, and other organizations. Increasingly, directors and managers of training and education operations are called upon to integrate new technologies into learning environments. They are expected to design, develop, and manage Web-based training initiatives even when they have little or no idea of what is involved in such activities. Our purpose in this book is to help those managers succeed.

Few people have all the skills and knowledge necessary to succeed at every task involved in a Web-based training program—nor should they have to be able to do everything. From our perspective, a successful manager's most crucial attributes are the ability and knowledge to oversee effectively a team of men and women who create, implement, and maintain an online learning environment. Throughout this book, our goal is to provide managers with enough awareness and understanding of all the aspects of a Web-based program that they can successfully oversee and manage it.

A major assumption of this book is that knowledge of technology alone is insufficient. As distance education expert Jay Alden has noted, "Too often we all become enamored with the technological capabilities of our bright and shiny devices and ignore fundamental learning theory." (Alden, 1998, p. ix.) For that reason, we spend time here (particularly in chapter 5) discussing the integration of sound learning principles into technology-based learning environments. Because we believe also that the true value of effective learning designs depends on the ability to implement them, we emphasize instructional systems design and human performance technology methods throughout the book.

The Web and other online technologies can provide us with powerful tools for training, but the possibilities can be overwhelming. One key to success is establishing specific objectives for the training program and remaining focused on the desired learning outcomes. The technology should assist you in meeting those objectives rather than create barriers or problems. We hope this book will help you maximize the benefits of technology in service of your training needs.

Acknowledgments

This book represents the collaborative efforts of many people in addition to the authors. We want to thank Steve Ackley, Chris Harper, Kathy Linstrum, Richard Kassissiah, Myron Maciejewski, and Robin Oliver for offering their professional expertise, content suggestions, and edits. We are indebted to Andrea Turner and Michael Starkman for providing information about the visual design and multimedia aspects of Web-based training and for creating many of the graphics we've included. We especially wish to thank Anne Derryberry and Informania, Inc., for their support of the book. Finally, we wish to acknowledge our appreciation to Mark Morrow, our editor at ASTD, for his support and commitment to the project.

Introduction

The Internet has changed the face of contemporary business. In doing so, it has changed how businesses operate and, in particular, how they access and share information. Organizations are scrambling to use the Internet and the World Wide Web in an effort to offer their workers access to information resources anywhere and at any time. The pace at which organizations have had to learn to leverage the Web to maintain a competitive edge has been phenomenal. In three years, the Internet went from a complex novelty to a global network connecting more than 90 million people and allowing them to communicate, exchange information, and do business around the world. The Internet's rate of growth is particularly impressive if you consider that it took radio more than 30 years to reach 60 million people and that it took television 15 years to reach the Internet's current levels of penetration.

The impact of the Internet on business makes understanding how to leverage the benefits of the Web a critical skill. This is especially true for those who manage how employees access information and training resources because of the many possibilities the Internet and the Web offer. Using the Web, training and development professionals can leverage instructional resources in ways never before possible.

The World Wide Web

The most important reason that the Internet has become such a powerful strategic commercial phenomenon is the World Wide Web, the fastest-growing segment of online activity for business. As recently as 1993, the Web was still considered an experimental concept. During the past five years, however, the Web has moved from an intriguing experiment in information technology to an essential part of how most companies conduct or plan to conduct business (see Figure 1.1).

How the Web Has Grown as a Training Vehicle

The Web's use of smaller-sized, less expensive, and more readily available technology is one of the most obvious benefits of Web-based training. Driving the growth of the Web as a training vehicle are these significant technology developments:

● **Computers are getting faster.** The processing power of today's desktop computers rivals that of large mainframe computers from only a decade ago. Those increases in speed and power greatly increase our ability to generate creative and productive solutions to job performance, and powerful, customizable, electronic performance improvement solutions, therefore, are within reach for organizations of all sizes and types.

● **Computers and networks communicate better.** Technology is solving the problem of getting different computers to "talk" with each other and share information. This means less energy focused on the tools of communication and networking and more on the business of sharing and using information.

Figure 1.1. Four stages of Internet development.

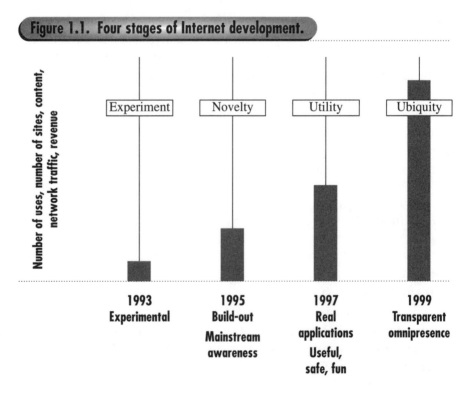

Adapted from R.H. Reid. (1997). *Architects of the Web: 1000 Days that Built the Future of Business* (p. xxxiv). Copyright © 1997 John Wiley & Sons. Reprinted by permission of John Wiley & Sons, Inc.

- **Browser technology is improving.** Browser software, such as Netscape and Internet Explorer, make it easy to make use of many of the latest developments in online multimedia. Ongoing developments in browser technology will make the use of such media for learning facilitation and professional development the rule rather than the exception. As long as sufficient bandwidth exists, such features as "streaming" audio and video, which transmit sounds, pictures, and motion in real time, will enable Web sites to offer real-time multimedia displays comparable to those available on a CD-ROM.

- **Computers are helping to manage knowledge.** New ways of storing data—whether text, animation, audio, or video—will allow trainers to select and compile just the right material for a training application. These *Knowledge Content Distributors,* or KCDs (Masie, 1998) as they are known, could radically alter how Web-based training is developed and managed.

- **Powerful new "intelligent" databases and search engines are being developed.** These new databases will enable users to access easily only the information that is relevant according to an individual, predetermined profile.

- **Accessing free information and buying services is increasingly easy.** The phenomenal proliferation of Web sites gives users previously unparalleled access to information and services. Although, the ".com" designation at the end of an Internet address for commercial Internet users has only been available since the privatization of the National Science Foundation's NSF-Net in the mid-1990s, the number of ".com" sites now exceeds all other designations. Previously, most Internet users were those affiliated with government and government-sponsored research organizations, educational institutions, and branches of the military.

- **Bandwidth is improving.** Transmission speeds in excess of one thousand times the current 28.8–56 kilobits per second (kbps) modem "standards" are likely to be available within the next few years. To put this in perspective, documents that now take 30 minutes to download to your hard drive may soon be captured in a matter of seconds.

Web Commerce

As reported in *Business Week*'s Information Technology Annual Report ("Doing Business," 1998), Forrester Research, Inc., estimates that goods and services sold online in 1998 will top $5.1 billion—more than double the figure for 1997. U.S. businesses will exchange an estimated $17 billion over the Internet in 1998, more than double the amount exchanged in 1997. By 2002, that number is expected to grow to $327 billion. As well as facili-

tating the explosive growth in online commerce, the Web has become a critical aspect of intracompany business activities, including professional development and training. Knowing how to use the World Wide Web effectively is required for those in the training and development field.

What Training Managers Need to Know

Recent developments in the Web have created revolutionary changes in the ways that training and development groups offer instruction and information to their organizations' employees. Training and performance support via the Web is only one of many technology-mediated learning applications collectively called "electronic learning" or learning technologies. Other technology-based training applications such as CD-ROMs and computer-based training are more familiar to most trainers and developers.

In their recent book, *ASTD Models for Learning Technologies: Roles, Competencies, and Outputs,* George M. Piskurich and Ethan S. Sanders (1998) divide learning delivered via technology into these major categories:

- instructional methods

- presentation methods

- distribution methods

The various components of each of those methods are presented in Table 1.1. That system of classification shows training practitioners the range of options available and provides a logical way of looking at the relationships among those technologies.

Table 1.1 Methods used for technology-delivered learning.

Instructional Methods
  Case study
  Demonstration
  Expert panels
  Games
  Group discussion
  Lecture
  Practical exercise
  Programmed instruction
  Reading
  Role play
  Simulation

Presentation Methods
  Audio
  Computer-based training
  Electronic text
  Electronic performance support
    systems
  Groupware

  Interactive TV
  Online help
  Teleconferencing
  3D modeling/virtual reality

Distribution Methods
  Audiotape
  Cable TV
  CD-ROM
  Computer disk
  Digital video disk
  Electronic mail
  Extranet, Internet, intranet
  LAN/WAN
  Satellite TV
  Tactile gear/simulator
  Telephone
  Videotape
  Voice mail
  World Wide Web

Adapted from G.M. Piskurich and E.S. Sanders. (1998). *ASTD Models for Learning Technologies: Roles, Competencies, and Outputs* (pp. 93–94). Alexandria, VA: American Society for Training & Development.

SECTION ONE

Building the Knowledge to Manage Web-Based Training

Chapter 1. Managing Web-Based Training

Effectively managing the design, development, and implementation of Web-based training will require all of your traditional training management skills plus a solid understanding of certain aspects of WBT technology. Because this technology can be complex, the common tendency is to focus exclusively on the technical processes and equipment, sometimes at the expense of more important components. Remember that proficiency with Web technology alone will not ensure the success of WBT resources and programs.

Effective WBT management also calls for an understanding of the needs and contributions of all the players involved, including Web designers and developers, content specialists, programmers, and artists. As a manager, you must ensure that the needs of your development team are synchronized with the needs of other essential staff involved in implementing the training. (The development staff will be discussed in detail in chapter 7). You may need to work with staff from these departments:

- information technology (IT)
- information systems (IS) and management information systems (MIS)
- product development
- human resources
- marketing and communications
- research and development
- engineering
- training, education, and professional development
- other departments with training needs

Each of those departments may have a stake in either what the program offers or how the training is put together and thus is a stakeholder in the project (see Practical Tip 1.1). For example, the IT and IS/MIS departments will have a vested interest in how the WBT program is integrated with the computer equipment in use in the organization and how the program will run on the existing network resources (hardware and software). Other departments will be interested in how information and training (content) related to their functions are presented in the program. For example, the product development and marketing departments will want to know that the training is consistent with how the company's products are positioned in the marketplace. Figure 1.1 depicts the primary focus of Web-based training for various departments.

Integrating Web-Based Training with Existing Training

Here are some more traditional learning approaches you may need to integrate with the Web-based program:

- face-to-face training (stand-up training)
- self-paced print resources
- audio and video programming
- computer-based training

Your program may include links to descriptions and schedules of classroom-based training, knowledge objects, database objects, and databases, as well as ordering information for print, CD-ROM, audiotape, and video resources.

The Impact of Web-Based Training on Users

The Web is a distribution channel with powerful capabilities that permit immediate dissemination of—and access to—audio, video, graphical, and textual information and interactivity. Furthermore, it is a communication

---

Practical Tips

1.1 Identifying Key Stakeholders

Use the following questions to help identify key stakeholders:
- Who, besides the training and development staff, currently develops training materials within the organization?
- Which departments use training materials?
- Has anyone indicated a need for training or performance improvement support?
- Who are the key supporters of training in your organization?
- Who should be involved in identifying hardware and software issues and in ensuring that the program is compatible with the equipment and software in use?
- Who will approve the program, including the development budget?

channel through which an infinite number of users can contact each other, either one-on-one or in groups, and in real time if they wish. The impact of this connection ability for training is monumental for several reasons:

● Training can be distributed quickly and easily to all members of the training audience.

● Training materials can be updated for a fraction of the cost of revising materials distributed by other means.

● Training requirements can drive the choice of media and learning strategies. For example, the training may be a self-paced, text-based exercise or a live video telecast.

● A geographically dispersed audience can communicate in real time with instructors, mentors, advisers, or colleagues.

● Immediate access to information resources or additional training can be made available. (To become familiar with some of the resources available on the Web, try Online Exercise 1, page 14.)

● Training-related functions such as registration, student tracking, and assessment can be conducted.

The benefits of this type of training include:

● greater engagement with subject matter

● sharing of solutions to problems

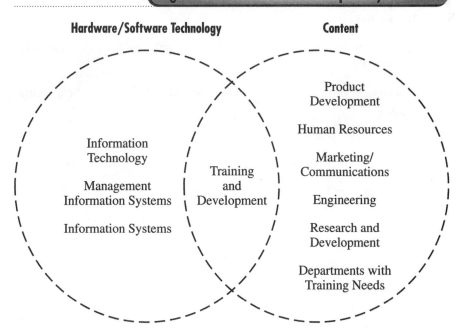

Figure 1.1. WBT stakeholders' primary concerns.

Hardware/Software Technology   Content

Information Technology

Management Information Systems

Information Systems

Training and Development

Product Development

Human Resources

Marketing/ Communications

Engineering

Research and Development

Departments with Training Needs

- synthesis of ideas

- spontaneous creativity

- greater feeling of connection with others in the target audience

Many of those benefits depend on developing learner-centered training materials; we will discuss learner-centered training in detail in chapter 3.

Attributes of an Effective Web-Based Training Program Manager

To manage each aspect of a WBT program successfully, you will need to call on your existing abilities and perhaps develop a few new areas of expertise. Here are some of the attributes that support successful management of WBT initiatives and programs:

- an ability to articulate the value that the Web brings to training and professional development

- a detailed understanding of the psychological effects of working in a virtual space

- an ability to align corporate culture and attitudes toward training and professional development with online learning

- a complete understanding of how offering WBT affects the organization

- a real appreciation of the constraints imposed by hardware and software on WBT efforts

- an understanding of the basic technological requirements for implementing WBT, including:

    ○ basics of connection speed (bandwidth) and random access memory (RAM)

    ○ computer processor types and their speed or information processing ability

    ○ how to use browsers, plug-ins, and extensions

    ○ differences in monitor resolution and display characteristics

    ○ database basics and methods for their integration

    ○ what is required for hosting a training site and issues relating to data security

    ○ basic concepts of the use of sound and video accelerator cards

    ○ how networks operate

- an appreciation for designing WBT systems oriented toward the needs of learners rather than the needs of instructors, training designers, or the technology

- the knowledge to use WBT when appropriate, such as when customized (individualized) course content supports training and performance goals

- the ability to determine when WBT is *not* the optimal solution

Checklist 1.1. Attributes of successful WBT managers.

Attribute	Self-Rating	Where Discussed in This Book
● Ability to define and present the value of WBT		Chapter 2
● Understanding of WBT's psychological effects on trainees		Chapter 3
● Ability to respond to corporate culture and attitudes about WBT		Chapter 3
● Understanding of WBT's organizational impact		Chapter 3
● Understanding of the constraints that hardware and software can impose		Chapter 4
● Understanding of the technological requirements		Chapter 4
● Ability to apply instructional design methods effectively to Web-based environments		Chapter 5
● Ability to determine the appropriateness of Web-based versus traditional training approaches		Chapter 5
● Ability to determine the appropriate features and benefits for the program		Chapter 6
● Understanding of staffing needs and effective team management		Chapter 7
● Ability to evaluate and maintain the Web site		Chapter 8

- a full understanding from a managerial perspective of what it takes to implement a WBT design, including staffing needs, the definition of new roles and responsibilities, and targeted outsourcing of specialized technical and support services

You can use Checklist 1.1 (page 7) to identify your current strengths as a manager of WBT and to determine the areas in which you need to gain greater experience or knowledge or draw on the experience of qualified staff members. For each of the attributes described in the table, use a rank-

Figure 1.2. Flowchart of WBT management activities.

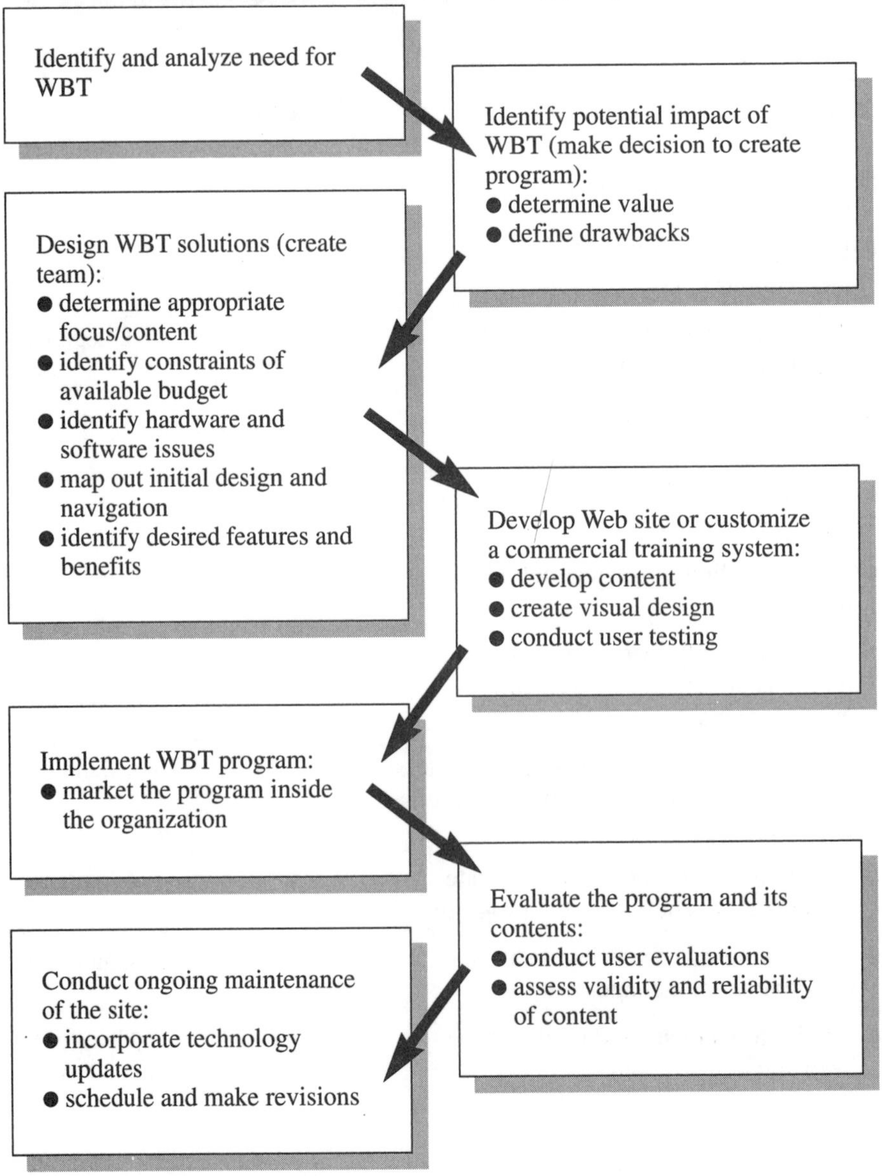

Identify and analyze need for WBT

Identify potential impact of WBT (make decision to create program):
- determine value
- define drawbacks

Design WBT solutions (create team):
- determine appropriate focus/content
- identify constraints of available budget
- identify hardware and software issues
- map out initial design and navigation
- identify desired features and benefits

Develop Web site or customize a commercial training system:
- develop content
- create visual design
- conduct user testing

Implement WBT program:
- market the program inside the organization

Evaluate the program and its contents:
- conduct user evaluations
- assess validity and reliability of content

Conduct ongoing maintenance of the site:
- incorporate technology updates
- schedule and make revisions

ing system that helps you measure how comfortable you are with your knowledge or ability to accomplish the associated task(s). The third column in the checklist indicates where in this book you will find the information you need to develop each attribute.

The ability to manage WBT projects effectively is becoming an essential skill for training professionals. Almost every aspect of business has been influenced by the growth of Internet-related technology and its use. Rapid technological innovation and the myriad uses of the Internet offer training professionals countless ways to harness the Web to support their organizations' training needs. Figure 1.2 is a flowchart of the major tasks you will undertake in managing WBT.

For an experiential perspective on those tasks and on WBT management in general, read the interview with a manager, which begins below. The interview introduces many of the issues we will discuss in this book.

Interview with a manager of WBT

A Cautionary Tale

The following interview was conducted with a manager who has developed several WBT programs.

Q: What is your background in project management, Web-based and otherwise?

A: I used to be a project manager in architectural design. Then I received my M.A. in instructional technology and now develop Web-based training.

Q: Can you describe your role as manager?

A: I oversee all phases of development. I supervise the instructional designers, programmers, subject matter experts, editors and quality assurance personnel, and the visual/creative staff. I'm the primary contact for outside vendors and internal customers, and I work with the business office for budgeting and financial issues. The only parts of the process where I am actually hands-on are the visual and interactive pieces.

Q: How is managing a Web-based project different from your previous experiences in project management?

A: The biggest difference is the technology. The great thing about technology is what it can do for the user; but from a managerial perspective, the technology imposes constraints and causes problems that paper-based projects don't have. For instance, if you're putting

continued on page 10

Interview, *continued*

together a project timeline, it's much easier to determine how long it
will take to develop a word-processed document or a blueprint than
it is to say just how long it will take to get a Web site fully functional. Also, the way I approach costs and budgeting is different. Development of Web-based training can get expensive and the expenses
tend to grow, so sometimes you don't have the budget to put in all
the functions and features you would like.

Q: Do you ever find you have to compromise the end product because
of the constraints you're talking about?

A: Yes and no. Yes, in the sense that you can't always do what you
want. In an ideal world, you could stick any function anywhere in a
Web site with little effort. And outsiders sometimes think anything is
possible! But the fact is that some functions and features take a
really long time to develop and will put you way over budget. So,
for example you may have to decide to cut down the number of
times you include animation. But, in a sense, the answer to your
question is also no because there are usually alternative ways to provide an effect similar to the original intent. There are a lot of software and other tools out there these days that can solve design problems. And the key thing is that even when you aren't able to include
all the bells and whistles you'd like, if it's still a great learning experience for the user, then you've achieved your goal.

Q: What is the biggest challenge you face?

A: The variety of end-user technology. It requires the team to spend a
lot of time ensuring compatibility with the different browsers, with
both PC and Mac platforms with different speed modems. What's
hard is not just the time it takes to accommodate end users' various
technologies; for the team members it's frustrating that what they
design may not necessarily be what the user sees, because of end-
user technology. This is especially true for the visual team. We
would all love to see more Web standards in place.

Q: Are there other challenges that are specific to Web-based training
projects?

A: Web-based projects tend to grow in scope and complexity over time.
You think you have a reasonable, relatively simple plan; then, sud-
denly, it's turned into a beast! As a manager, it's important to be able
to recognize when a project is getting out of control. The goal is to
deliver a product in a timely manner, so you need to bring people
back to reality sometimes. Also, however, you need to be flexible so

that if the project does grow in good ways with unexpected changes, you are ready.

Q: But, practically speaking, how can a project manager be *ready* for unexpected changes?

A: Well, there are changes and then there are *changes*. Some changes are easy, like updating content and adding quizzes or Web links. Other changes in the basic structure of the program are nearly impossible, like building a house and then deciding you want to change the foundation completely after you start shingling the roof. In terms of being ready for changes, there are a few things you can do. First, get enough time in your schedule and money in your budget for changes so that it's not a catastrophe if there have to be alterations. Second, think of "what-if" scenarios, such as What if the marketing department decides it wants this module to interface with its database using a password? You can't think of everything, but it will help to have a mindset in which you're ready to deal with special requests. And third, expect to be asked to cross-purpose any learning product you develop—for example, to convert it to a CD-ROM or a sound clip. You should keep any original files you might need later for cross-purposing. Finally, make sure things are signed off and approved at each stage. Make sure the team and key stakeholders are happy before moving to the next stage. This will prevent your having to go back and make complicated changes that could have been dealt with before the site got more complex.

Q: What about the team—is teamwork any different on this kind of project?

A: Because of the technology, each person's task is usually related to or dependent on someone else's work. So the team is really interconnected. One person out of the loop can mess up the whole process. For example, if you're developing a series of quizzes, there are a number of questions that involve not only the instructional designers but also the visual designers, multimedia experts, and programmers. Questions such as "Do you want to use check boxes or radio buttons?" [Check boxes enable the user to select more than one option in a multiple-choice quiz; radio buttons offer only one choice.] What kind of feedback do you want the user to get? How comprehensive and fast should it be? Will you need CGI [common gateway interface] programming? Until these things are decided, visual can't design the layout, and the instructional designers can't establish content and instructions. The same holds true for audio

continued on page 12

Interview, *continued*

considerations. Do you want audio to be automatic, or should the
user have to click for it? This decision will affect nearly everyone.

Q: As a manager, how do you deal with this increased interdependence
of team members?

A: Try to maximize time and plan so that people aren't just waiting
around for others to finish their portion. Make all these functionality
decisions early on so that time isn't wasted waiting for a decision.
Sometimes you will need the whole team in a room together to talk
about the project. But this drains your budget, so you should do as
much one-on-one as possible. In a meeting, set an agenda, stick to it,
set a maximum time, and stay focused. Don't force the whole team
to sit in on a conversation about CGI that you could have just with
the programmer.

Q: So, what are some of the benefits or things you particularly like
about managing Web-based training?

A: Web-based projects get done. That's very satisfying. There is a sense
of urgency in Web-based design. The whole philosophy of the Web
is access to information *now!* Plus, people know that technology
constantly changes, so they want to get the site fully functional
quickly. Then, over time, you can tweak and maintain it in response
to changes.

Q: You said the urgency of Web-based design is partly the result of
constant technological changes. Do you have any suggestions for
how to anticipate these changes?

A: Stay abreast of the industry. Give yourself a little time each week for
research and development. Subscribe to relevant journals and e-mail
distribution lists, or bookmark relevant Web sites. Familiarize yourself with new advancements and trends. You don't have to know
everything, but try to learn the basics and stay tuned in.

Q: Where do you think Web-based training will go in the future?

A: Well, I would hope that compatibility issues would go away, but I
think that there always will be competing companies whose different
products cause compatibility problems. I'm glad to see a push
toward standards in some areas—for example, the 216-color palette
[there are 216 colors that Internet Explorer reads the same as
Netscape]. In terms of the role of Web-based training, I think companies will start using intranets more for their training, and they will
be creating better interfaces between their intranets and the Web. I
think also that with improved monitoring capabilities, there will be

more monitoring of employee performance on competencies training. This trend could bring both negative and positive results. The negative impulse might be to turn monitoring into a watchdog or Big Brother function. That can harm learner motivation, and it brings up legal issues. But the positive side is that monitoring can help us measure results better. Companies want to know that their training investments are paying off, and learners will want effective programs constructed to help them in their performance and career advancement.

Q: What advice would you give somebody who is about to start managing his or her first Web-based training project?

A: Be ready to make a mental shift. You're dealing with a new medium. Not only are there new possibilities for users, but users also have different expectations than they have of other kinds of training. They expect the Web to stimulate them. From a user's perspective, your site will be competing with thousands of others on the Web. And many of those are high-end commercial sites. Don't forget that much of the Web is about advertising, so the look and functionality of your site will be very important. Another piece of advice is to learn each team member's role. You don't have to know how they do everything, but you need to know what they do. Interview them and take notes if necessary. You will need all the soft skills you normally use in project management. You're still dealing with people who have emotions and egos and need positive reinforcement and recognition. My final word of advice is not to worry. You'll be fine. You're building on skills you already have!

Online Exercise 1. Using online resources.

One of the Web's greatest benefits is its ability to provide access to vast databases of information. The amount of information can be overwhelming, however, and you may become frustrated in your search for specific information. This online exercise illustrates the frustration that you may experience when the amount of information available exceeds your needs. It will help you understand the need to be careful in selecting the information resources you include in your WBT program and the importance of guiding the user through the site. You also may experience some of the potential disadvantages that an online tool presents, such as time delays. Finally, if you are relatively unfamiliar with the Web, this exercise will introduce you to the use of online resources.

To begin, you will need to open your browser (for example, Netscape or Internet Explorer).

- **The Unguided Search**
  Your goal is to find out as much as possible about a commercial training system (in this case, Oracle Training Plan Builder).

Step 1
  In the "go to" section at the top of your browser, type: www.yahoo.com (or www.lycos. com, www.excite.com, www.infoseek.com, and so forth) or press the "Search" button.

Step 2
  In the "search for" box, type: Oracle

Step 3
  Scroll through the various search results and click on the link that seems to correspond to the site at which you would find a demonstration of the Training Plan Builder. If the site does not offer what you are looking for, click on the "back" button on your browser and choose another link. Continue this process until you find what you are looking for (or decide to give up the search).

Unguided Search Questions
- How easily where you able to identify a site that offered information about the system?
- Were you frustrated in your search?
- If you were frustrated in your search, how were you frustrated?
  - Did you encounter any "404 File Not Found" messages? If not, have you encountered this message before? How did it make you feel?

Note: A "404 File Not Found" message indicates that the link is no longer active. Most WBT programs have multiple links to learning resources. Imagine the negative perception about the reliability of the program and the amount of frustration that are created when a user clicks on a link and is told that the linked resource is no longer available.

○ Did you feel that the number of matches made the search more difficult than it needed to be?

○ Was an online demonstration offered at the site? Once you found the appropriate site, was it easy to access the simulation/demonstration of the product?

○ In what other ways was the experience frustrating (for example, time delays, seemingly inappropriate links)?

● **The Guided Search**

In the unguided search, you had all the resources associated with Oracle available to you. In this search, you will be guided directly to those resources associated only with Training Plan Builder.

Step 1

Type: www.oracle.com.sg/education/
[In the unguided search, were you able to find these Web pages?]

Step 2

Type one of the following: www.informania.com/what/products/index.html
www.asymetrix.com/products/librarian/index.html

Step 3

Take the guided tour or simulation that is offered.

Guided Search Questions

● How much easier was your search with the specific links?

● How much less frustrating was it to be guided directly to the information you wanted?

● How did the experience of taking the guided tour or simulation differ from making a relatively unguided search for information?

Note: At the time of publication, the links listed in this book led to the specific information noted. If you come across a link that is no longer active, please go to www.informania.com/managingwbt. If you find no replacement link listed, fill out the feedback form to let us know that the link is no longer functional.

Chapter 2. Assessing the Benefits and Drawbacks of Web-Based Training

The increasingly complex and competitive nature of the workplace has led to increased demands for better access to information to support learning and performance. Even small organizations now are able to provide instant training and performance support because the hardware, software, and connection infrastructure (that is, local area and wide area networks) are affordable and available. Although many organizations have adopted WBT enthusiastically, in the planning phase they do not always have a methodology for assessing the appropriateness, potential advantages, and drawbacks of its implementation. This chapter compares the benefits and risks of WBT to those of traditional training and provides a return-on-investment model for assessing those benefits, defining their value, and presenting them to key stakeholders and others in your organization.

Demand for Performance Improvement in the Workplace

As discussed in chapter 1, rapid developments in technology have made WBT accessible to organizations of various sizes and characters. Remember, however, that WBT adoption should be fueled by organizational needs, not by the availability of astonishing new technologies. Today, many organizations are seeking to bring about individual performance improvement in the most effective and efficient ways. Workers need access to resources that help them evaluate business scenarios and recognize and solve problems in a rapidly changing business environment. Several factors drive this need: intense global competition in businesses that once held a domestic monopoly; the new, central role of knowledge in our economy; and the rush by companies to gain a technological edge. Because those are the challenges that WBT is uniquely positioned to meet, training and development departments increasingly are offering learning resources online in an effort to improve worker performance.

Why Conventional Training Often Is Not Sufficient

Today more than ever, the training needs of organizations extend beyond classroom instruction. Conventional classroom-based training often is unable to provide the continuous, individualized learning and performance improvement that electronic media such as the Web can offer. This situation exists because, in many cases, conventional training is not developed proactively to meet a company's strategic business needs. Rather, it has been implemented in a reactive mode, in response to a performance deficiency. An example of this kind of training is product training designed as a remedy for a perceived lack of knowledge. Such training might typically ask salespeople or customer service representatives to learn facts about the product and then to complete a set of tasks using the new information. WBT also can be used in that way—simply to address performance deficiencies. However, it also enables learners to seek out instantly available resources proactively, when and where the users need them.

To continue with the example of product training used above, WBT can be structured to mirror the offerings of conventional classroom training (for example, an introduction to new information, opportunities for practice, and testing). But it offers trainees much more: instant access to a vast array of online resources, such as databases; competitors' product information (for example, prices, marketing materials, technical specifications); government regulations; academic research; breaking news in the field; and real-time communication with other trainees, instructors, or field professionals. Those resources can be incorporated item-by-item into the training, in accordance with individual learner needs.

A related problem with conventional training is that it is difficult to offer continuous learning opportunities in traditional formats. Learning is formalized and scheduled for specific beginning and ending times. Because of access limitations, learning may be viewed as a one-shot opportunity or a biannual event. WBT, however, provides learners with continuous learning options. Learning can take place 15 minutes every day if that schedule suits the learner's continuous training and scheduling needs. Continuous learning can be crucial in business environments in which the pace of change is rapid.

Conventional classroom-based training requires physical presence, a requirement that can be costly in terms of both travel expense and lost time spent traveling. Even if travel is not required, employees who work at a distance from the office may be denied training opportunities. Distance learning and computer-based training have addressed the needs of distance learners. WBT brings them even closer, with the added functionality and stimulation of real-time online communication and instant information.

A final deficiency of conventional training is the difficulty of integrating such training with performance support. Although they are related, training and performance support are not the same thing. As a practice, training targets specific knowledge, skills, or competencies; performance support tries to improve how workers do their jobs by taking into account a wider range of factors that influence performance. Such interventions often include training, but they also can focus on nontraining organizational influences, such as access to information on the job, the work environment, or the usability of job aids. In chapter 9, we discuss performance support more fully and introduce the performance improvement environment.

The gap between training and performance support is wider in conventional training than in WBT, rendering the training less effective or less relevant than it could be. For example, the information in conventional training materials may quickly become outdated, and those materials thus become ineffective performance support tools. Also, paper-based training materials, such as a binder with work sheets and tables, are unwieldy tools compared with an online program that, for example, teaches trainees how to identify potential customers through Web-based research. WBT can operate easily as a performance support tool because of the adaptability and flexibility of its content and structure. Therefore, WBT can integrate training and performance support seamlessly to an extent nearly impossible with conventional training.

In summary, WBT's accessibility, timeliness, and interactive nature can help meet a much wider range of training objectives than can conventional training. That kind of flexibility is increasingly crucial in today's fast-changing business environment and is difficult to provide in the conventional classroom.

Is Web-Based Training Always the Answer?

Despite its benefits, WBT may not always be the most efficient or effective approach to training and performance improvement. In some cases, it may make sense to continue using only conventional training or to create a hybrid program that combines conventional and Web-based training. Being capable of assessing the benefits and drawbacks of WBT in your organization (especially when you are asked to justify the costs associated with the initial implementation of such training) is a vital management skill. To assist you in that task, the following two sections discuss the advantages and drawbacks of WBT compared with those of conventional training (see Table 2.1).

Advantages of Web-Based Training

Training Is Learner Centered

WBT is more learner centered than is conventional classroom-based training, which is often seen as something "done to" the learners. In traditional training, because specific outcomes must be achieved, learners are expected to conform to a path dictated by the designer of the learning experience, the instructor, or both. Typically, traditional training is not flexible enough to meet an individual's specific learning needs. The training also may not be

Table 2.1. Comparative advantages.

Web-Based Training	Classroom-Based Training
● Addresses learning at the individual level.	● Addresses learning in a group context.
● Can be designed for use anytime and anywhere.	● Must be scheduled for a time and a location.
● Maximizes connections among learner(s) and resources.	● May be limited by resources physically present.
● Can be designed to be learner-driven at a pace that corresponds to an individual's learning style.	● Moves at a pace set by the group.
● Can be used at the trainee's job site, as time is available.	● May require travel and time away from the trainee's regular job.
● Makes it possible to access resources quickly and easily at any time through online search engines.	● Content is tied to the classroom setting or to predetermined, prepared materials.
● May require less of an investment in on-site instructors.	● May require a significant investment in training personnel to deliver training.
● Does not require additional physical space.	● Requires physical space.
● Connects learners in diverse locations.	● Addresses participants only in the same physical space.
● Enables immediate implementation of new learning.	● Implementation of learning can be overridden by crises at hand.
● Facilitates seamless connection between training and performance support.	● Training and performance support are more likely to be approached as separate efforts.

available when a learner most needs it. In contrast, WBT provides learners with an opportunity for improvement wherever an Internet connection or a network connection can be made. Because it can be used by learners in so many places and, generally, with a variety of end-user equipment, WBT offers much greater access than do older, computer-based training models. In chapter 5, we discuss traditional versus learner-centered instructional approaches in greater detail.

Individual Learners' Needs Are Accommodated

Classroom-based training addresses learning needs in a group context; well-designed WBT focuses on the needs of individuals looking for immediate access to instructional opportunities, performance support tools, or information. Conventional training must be scheduled in advance, and it typically moves at the pace set by the group rather than by the individual. WBT is available when and where it is needed, at times and in formats that serve the precise needs of the individual.

Geographically Dispersed Learners Connect

WBT can provide connections between and among learners and resources in various physical locations. As such, it maximizes the connections between people at multiple locations and resources that may be housed at one or more other locations. Given such components as chat rooms, e-mail, and interactive Web pages, where learners and resources are physically situated is irrelevant. What is relevant is that the two connect in a highly stimulating manner. Online conversations can be exciting because people from diverse locations contribute. Real-time communication is especially energizing for many people, and it helps reduce the isolation that users can feel when dialing into the site from a distance.

Rapid Individualized Assessments Can Be Made

Traditional training approaches often incorporate individualized assessment, but WBT increases the opportunities to determine and immediately respond to individual needs. Web-based learning tools can create a learner profile and instantly direct users to the resources that will address their skill gaps and professional development needs most effectively. Those WBT attributes let users monitor their own progress and determine the next steps in their professional development.

Content Can Be Adapted and Updated Continuously

In WBT, content is not tied to a classroom setting or to preprinted materials. Online search engines make it possible to access resources quickly and easily at any time. Content can be adapted to individual skill level, job function, and learning style. WBT also provides the most up-to-date content because electronic information can be updated every minute. Asking workshop participants in traditional settings to replace outdated pages in their binders, for example, is a much more disruptive and time-consuming way to update printed information.

Just-in-Time Learning Is Delivered

Just-in-time (JIT) training is delivered exactly as learners need it: at precisely the time and with exactly the content required. The just-in-time, just-for-me model has been embraced by many people in the instructional design field for two reasons. First, in an era of leaner training departments, just-in-time learning reduces the time and cost of designing, delivering, and following formal training programs; it does so through such strategies as using templates, delivering only the most immediately pertinent material, and shifting some instructional design responsibilities to the trainee. Second, and more important, the just-in-time approach posits individual needs as the starting point for determining when and how training will be delivered, rather than forcing individuals to accommodate themselves to predetermined times and content. For both of those reasons, adding a JIT strategy to the overall training program can improve an organization's ability to respond to competitive pressures significantly.

WBT strongly promotes the move in the training field toward JIT learning. Because it is an interactive medium, the Web offers an ideal way to respond to unique just-in-time, just-for-me training and information needs of individuals and organizations, regardless of their physical locations.

Training Programs Are More Likely to Be Implemented

In a traditional training program, the crises of the moment interfere with the best intentions to make use of the instruction. Goals set as part of a training experience are set aside to deal with the day-to-day details of business and often are not implemented at all. In a traditional off-site training program with printed materials created specifically for the program, the training is usually constructed as an event in which the time, place, and materials are unique to the training experience (that is, they are not part of the learner's actual job activities).

WBT, however, can be constructed so that training is a form of learning on the job. A manual or handbook may provide on-the-job training, but neither medium offers anything that approaches the Web's ability to help the learner locate essential job-performance resources immediately, both online and offline. Those resources may be accessed repeatedly in the future to help the learner make decisions or to promote professional growth. Furthermore, for the ever-increasing number of workers who use the Internet on the job, WBT lets them learn with a tool they use regularly rather than with a set of materials they may never use again. Thus, the medium of WBT facilitates implementation of skills and knowledge in a way that classroom-based training often cannot.

Travel Costs, Lost Work Hours, and Revision Charges Are Reduced

Conventional training can incur high costs for travel and lodging expenses time away from productive work and other expenses such as tuition or registration fees. WBT also can be costly to implement, but it can save the company a good deal of money both in the travel budget and in productivity. Furthermore, content revisions can be costly in print-based or video-based learning. Minor content changes on a Web site, however, are generally quick and easy to perform at minimal cost.

Potential Drawbacks of Web-Based Training

Despite WBT's many benefits, several potential drawbacks must be considered before an implementation decision is made.

Online Activity May Be Time Consuming

The primary disadvantage is the potential for lags in response time. Those lags may result from a high volume of Internet traffic or from bandwidth issues (for example, users connecting via a modem at home may find the downloading of larger files particularly slow).

Additional Software May Be Needed

Plug-ins and extensions can complicate both the development and use of a program, especially if the learner has to take extra time or needs assistance in downloading them. The variety of browsers and operating systems that learners are using to access the training can make the design as it appears on the developers' machines look quite different on the users' machines. In chapter 4, we will discuss software issues in greater detail.

Initial Implementation Can Be Costly

The initial development and implementation of WBT can be very expensive, even prohibitively so for some organizations. In the short term, conventional training may be less costly. If the need for training is not strong across the organization, implementing an expensive WBT program may not be a good idea.

People May Feel Disenfranchised

An electronic learning system, when implemented entirely in place of traditional classroom-based training, can cause people to feel disconnected from the organization, especially if they are mobile workers. That feeling can lead to decreased productivity, morale problems, and higher turnover. The sense of disenfranchisement can be offset by other organizational programs that enhance worker–organization connection, but those programs will probably incur costs (Derryberry, 1998).

Optimal Site and Functionality Can Be Difficult to Define

One of the biggest barriers to implementing WBT programs lies in planning and establishing appropriate Web site size (sometimes referred to as the "real estate") and functionality. Functionality refers to the features offered at the site. The sizes and functions of Web sites can vary dramatically, depending on the kinds of operations to be accomplished there. As organizations begin their forays into WBT, there is a tendency to forget that the requirements for designing a simple Web site are quite unlike those needed to design and implement a large-scale WBT initiative. The more complex the site, the more staffing and financial resources you will need. In a smaller organization, the need for more resources over time may make it more difficult to justify implementing WBT. In chapter 4, we address size and functionality concerns from a technological perspective.

Determining the Appropriateness of Web-Based Training

The preceding discussion of WBT's potential benefits and drawbacks was intended to help you decide if WBT is appropriate for your organization. Practical Tip 2.1 presents questions to guide you in deciding whether to implement such a program and in assessing the challenges you may face as you introduce it, and Practical Tip 2.2 presents WBT's performance benefits.

Practical Tips

2.1 Is a WBT Program Your Answer?

Consider your organization's answers to these questions before committing resources to developing a WBT program.
- What is the nature of the performance deficiency or the learning opportunity that the intended program is expected to address? What are some of the attributes of the targeted deficiencies or opportunities?
- Is instruction or training the most appropriate intervention to achieve anticipated results? Would a performance support solution work just as well as or better than instruction or training? Are both required? Is the

Practical Tip, *continued*

core of the performance problem related to a need to build knowledge, skills, and competencies among the targeted audience? Is the real need related to information access?

● To what degree can technology respond to the identified deficiencies or opportunities? To what degree can it be used in lieu of existing methods of supporting organizational performance improvement?

● Who is the target audience? Are they site-bound or mobile? If site-bound, are they at a single location or campus, or are they dispersed across multiple locations? Are they members of existing cohort groups? Will they collectively constitute a new cohort group, or are they likely to demand services and resources as individual users?

● Every project has a budget. Is this one fixed or flexible? In other words, if increasing the project budget to include interactive technology could ultimately save or make more money for the organization, could additional funds be made available to support the project?

● Who else will benefit from this solution? What is the "trickle-down" or ripple effect of this project? If others benefit, should those others pay their share?

● Is the person to whom you are making your business case the one who can approve the program's development?

● What if the solution you recommend is different from what is requested or expected? What can you do if your recommendation exceeds the current budget?

● Who are the real decision makers? Sometimes the gatekeeper (that is, the person designated to deal with project-specific personnel, resources, and overall project management) may not be the decision maker. Sometimes the designated decision maker is simply representing the interests of the key stakeholder.

● Is interactive technology currently available in this setting? How widespread is it?

● If interactive technology is available, what kinds of resources are available to users currently? What resources are planned?

● Are those resources developed by commercial vendors? Are they developed by a custom design firm? Are they developed internally? To what kinds of standards or protocols do they adhere?

Source: Adapted from Derryberry, A. (1998). "Making the Business Case: Predicting ROI for Performance Improvement Environment and Electronic Learning." In *Learning Without Limits* (volume 2, pp. 35–48). San Francisco: Informania. Used with permission.

Resistance to Web-Based Training

Many compelling arguments can be made to demonstrate that WBT adds value. Nonetheless, there remains some resistance to its full-scale, enterprise-wide implementation. For example, in a fall 1996 survey conducted by researchers at Georgia Tech University, 85 percent of respondents from *Fortune* 500 companies indicated that their companies had either implemented or were in the process of implementing companywide intranets. But only 68 percent of those respondents said that WBT efforts were likely to be implemented in the next six to 18 months (Pitkow and Recker, 1996). The American Society for Training & Development's *State of the Industry Report* for 1998 noted that training delivered via corporate intranets was used for only 3 percent of the respondents' total training efforts. Electronic performance support systems were used in 7 percent of the training offered by companies participating in the study (Bassi and Van Buren, 1998), in contrast to the more than 80 percent of training interventions that continue to be made available in face-to-face classroom settings.

Remember that WBT is a relatively new feature on the training and development landscape, and resistance to it may reflect an uncertainty about how to leverage the unique features that it offers individuals and organizations. Many organizations are still having a hard time imagining how business processes can be reengineered for deployment using technology-based delivery options like the Web. The resistance may also result from inappro-

Practical Tips

2.2 Describing the Performance Benefits of WBT

Web-based training:
- facilitates the proactive use of resources by users
- is learner centered and enables individuals to be self-directed and to manage their own professional development
- makes it easier to track down resources when and where they are needed
- offers individualized assessments that direct the learner to those resources that most effectively meet a current professional development need
- provides opportunities for real-time communication with peers or other learners in geographically dispersed locations

priate expectations that have been placed on Web-based media. For example, some training experts are disturbed that WBT blurs the lines between training and performance support and that WBT therefore does not qualify as "training" in the traditional sense (Filipczak, 1996). In 1998, instructional design pioneer M. David Merrill warned that the Internet is not a learning medium per se, and that "students like to get on the Internet and jump all around. But if you want serious learning, the Internet (and its general content) is pretty shallow. There isn't enough guidance and structure there for someone to learn a systematic body of knowledge" ("Wake Up!" 1998). To argue that WBT is insufficient as a training solution because it differs fundamentally from more traditional models is somewhat circular logic. If WBT were not fundamentally different, it would be hard to justify or rationalize implementing it as a training approach to replace or supplement existing programs. Obviously, being different does not mean that WBT is a poor substitute for traditional approaches any more than it means that it is fundamentally better than traditional methods.

Making the Case: Assessing Return-on-Investment of a Web-Based Training Program

Overcoming resistance to WBT can be difficult, but you can make a much stronger case if you demonstrate that you understand and have weighed the costs and benefits associated with such a program. There are many ways to prepare and present a cost-benefit analysis. The resources section at the end of this book lists some publications you may wish to consult if you are preparing such a report. There are also several software programs to use in generating a cost-benefit analysis. In general, your analysis must include all of the quantifiable costs your organization will incur in all stages of training (design, development, and delivery).

One form of cost-benefit analysis that often is used in assessing educational technology is return-on-investment. ROI analysis seeks to demonstrate that a program or intervention has a direct positive impact on an organization's competitiveness and productivity (Derryberry, 1998). The term *ROI* is used to designate benefits that are both quantitative (measurable in monetary value) and qualitative (less tangible or less measurable, but still capable of affecting the bottom line). Quantitative ROI analysis (whether of a training program or any other financial investment) is based on a formula in which earnings are divided by investment:

$$\text{ROI} (\%) = \frac{\text{earnings}}{\text{investment}} \times 100$$

The result will be a percentage. For example, if you invest $100 and you earn $200, your ROI will be 100 percent. In the case of training, the ROI formula is

$$ROI\ (\%) = \frac{\text{net training benefits}}{\text{training costs}} \times 100$$

Net training benefits are determined by subtracting training costs from training benefits. For instance, imagine that you invest $10,000 in WBT. You find that over the next year, you will save $7,000 in travel expenses and $3,000 in wages to hire temporary workers to stand in for employees who are at training. The training also results in increased sales and productivity estimated to be worth $10,000. Your net training benefit will be $10,000 ($20,000 benefit minus $10,000 initial investment), so your ROI is 100 percent. (The costs and benefits in that example are simplified for the sake of clarity. When projecting the full costs of WBT, refer to Practical Tip 6.1, on page 78, as well as to the descriptions of benefits and drawbacks presented earlier in this chapter.

The basic ROI formula is simple to use for many kinds of investments, but preparing an accurate ROI for training can be difficult. Although there are case studies of WBT ROI, assessing the total costs and benefits of a performance improvement program is challenging in most cases because there is no one-to-one correspondence between the training offerings and increased revenues and productivity. Furthermore, it can be difficult to determine exactly which and how much of dispersed organizational expenses are associated with the development of a training program (see Practical Tip 2.3).

Practical Tips

2.3 Describing the Financial and Organizational Benefits of WBT

Web-based training:
- reduces or eliminates travel expenses for training
- reduces the amount of time trainees must spend away from work
- reduces the cost of updating and distributing training materials
- allows for greater flexibility in scheduling training
- connects learners in various locations
- can incorporate technology that is already owned but underused
- standardizes training across the organization

Although it also is inherently difficult to measure the long-term or intangible benefits of training in terms of precise monetary values, it is possible to develop ROI information that supports training projects such as a WBT program. The discussion here is intended to help you prepare a more accurate presentation of ROI information than a simple formula permits. You will need to consider a number of costs:

● the purchase of new equipment and equipment upgrades over time

● Web site development, including the time-on-task for the development team, programmer analysts, subject matter experts, beta testers, and quality assurance staff

● end-user technical support costs

● telephone and network access and service charges

● paper and printing costs for making hard copies of electronic documents

● ongoing maintenance and revision of the Web site

On the benefits side, a WBT program may provide

● usage of owned but underused technology

● standardized, interactive, technology-based training and/or support that enhances consistency of training across the organization

● reduced trainee downtime compared with the time needed for other types of training

● reduced expenses in delivering training and in bringing people to the training (that is, lower instructor, training site, and travel costs)

● reduced cost of updating and distributing training materials and information

In addition, effective WBT and performance support programs can lead to somewhat less tangible benefits that are more difficult to relate directly to the program. Nevertheless, qualitative benefits are worth mentioning as part of a WBT ROI analysis:

● **Reduced turnover:** In situations in which high turnover results from a perceived lack of opportunity, a WBT program can offer employees the opportunity to develop their skills and can open up new avenues of growth for them in the organization. The related cost savings can be determined if the full costs of hiring, training, outfitting, and supporting replacement personnel can be calculated accurately. If the human resources department can provide you with only the estimated costs of turnover, it is worth mentioning that a WBT program can help reduce those costs even if you cannot definitively indicate the amount of the cost savings.

● **Improved morale:** Organizations that experience low morale because employees perceive they are not highly valued can correct that perception by investing in performance improvement programs such as WBT. If workers identify training as an investment in their development, their morale and productivity are likely to rise.

● **Increased use of training and support programs:** By making an investment in electronic learning or a performance improvement environment, an organization signals the importance and value it places on training, support, and professional development. This, in turn, can motivate employees to avail themselves of those resources and enhance their individual value to the organization.

● **Competitive advantage gained through use of leading-edge interventions:** Until interactive technology is the norm, organizations that adopt it for employee development will be recognized as being on the leading edge. Often, the cachet that accompanies this perception is the belief that such an organization provides innovative products and services to the marketplace (Derryberry, 1998).

There is a limited amount of research to draw on in presenting those intangible benefits. One of the first studies to make the long-term benefits of training more tangible and quantifiable was the *1998 ASTD State of the Industry Report* (Bassi and Van Buren, 1998), which drew a connection between high-performance, leading-edge organizations and their strong commitment to training. The report demonstrates that there is a significant gap between the training investment that high-performing companies make and the training investment that all other companies make.

In preparing an ROI report, you probably will not be able to include in the ROI formula the qualitative benefits defined above. When you make ROI projections, however, present to your audience the less tangible considerations as well as the quantitative ones. One way you can present your projections is to separate quantitative from qualitative considerations. First present the quantitative information, with written explanations of the costs and benefits accompanying a table of costs and expenses and the ROI formula with its final return in percentage form. Follow that with a second section that discusses or presents as bullet points the less tangible but equally important qualitative considerations. Online Exercise 2 can help you focus your thinking with regrd to how WBT can benefit your organization.

▼ ▼ ▼

You must be able to assess and define the value of WBT for your organization for two reasons. First, you will have to determine whether it is currently the right training path for your organization and, if so, how extensive the initial training program should be. Clearly, that decision will require a thorough understanding of the benefits and drawbacks of such a program as they relate to your company's specific needs. Second, you must sell the training program to others in your organization. Whether you take the ROI approach or another model, the success or failure of your proposal may depend largely on your ability to demonstrate an understanding of the costs and benefits associated with such training.

Online Exercise 2. Benefits and drawbacks of WBT.

● The following Web site offers a good description of WBT's potential advantages and disadvantages: www.esocrates.com

Question

● Are the potential advantages and disadvantages described at the site relevant to your organization's training situation? If so, how might you capitalize on the benefits and minimize or account for the potential drawbacks?

Note: If the above link is no longer active, use one or more of the Web search engines (for example, Excite, Yahoo!, Lycos, Infoseek, Alta Vista, or WebCrawler) to find recent Web documents that focus on WBT, or visit Informania's site (www.informania.com/managingwbt) for updated directions.

ter 3. Unique Considerations for Web-Based Learning

...menting Web-based learning, you will ...u would not normally have to address in ...aches. For training developers and ...eriences may not look like or work like ...ady know. Some people may object to ... as good as what they have experienced ...classroom. One of your more significant challenges will be to alter any of the negative perceptions about online learning that exist in your organization. This can be accomplished by focusing on the unique charac-teristics of WBT, describing how online learning can complement an overall performance support program, and effectively addressing areas of concern. To do so, you will need to consider the following four general issues:

1. Learner Motivation

What impact will an online training environment have on learners' moti-vation? Will the motivation to learn specific material be enhanced or suffer when using an online delivery approach?

2. Corporate Culture and Attitudes

What attitudes do members of your organization have toward training and, in particular, online learning? How might current attitudes about the use of online resources affect attitudes toward online training?

3. Course Design Strategies

How can you develop courses that facilitate online learning and support a learner-centered approach? How can the design of online courses enhance learner motivation and the desire to learn and apply knowledge?

4. Constraints Imposed by Hardware and Software

What constraints do the operating systems, hardware, and other software in use in your organization impose on a WBT program? Do the hardware and software in use support the online features necessary to develop courses that promote learning?

Learner Motivation

WBT programs require that learners be self-motivated. Just as people differ in their motivation to perform their job responsibilities, they also differ in their motivation to learn and in their drive to develop professionally. Some people are highly motivated, regardless of the specific circumstances, and they seek ways to learn in almost any learning environment. They may be the first to embrace a WBT program because it allows them to exhibit greater control and self-direction and to act in a motivated fashion. However, other people are slower to accept change and to see the opportunities that a new approach offers them. Perhaps the greatest challenges with any new learning initiative are to sell the value of the approach to users and to increase their motivation to use it. Because WBT is new to most users, it requires that you sell it effectively to the end users and help them see how the program will benefit them.

Differences in individual motivation also affect willingness to continue work on a task (Kanfer, 1993; Miceli and Lane, 1991; Steers and Porter, 1989). Because most Web-based programs rely on learner initiative to access and make use of online resources, differences in motivation and persistence will affect how workers respond to a WBT program. If users are not motivated to use the program, the time and money spent developing the site will be wasted. As you develop WBT resources, it is critical to understand how they may affect the learner's motivation to use them and how they may ultimately determine the success or failure of the program. For example, does the design decrease a learner's motivation to use the program? You should assess motivation as part of all user testing components (as discussed in later chapters). Here are some basic findings regarding learner motivation:

● Motivation increases when learners believe that a training experience will make learning easier and that learning will lead to better performance.

● Motivation increases when people believe that better performance will be recognized and rewarded.

● Motivation increases when workers value the rewards that come from better performance (Blair and Price, 1998).

Thus, the first challenge in motivating learners is to help them understand how a WBT program will assist them in improving their performance. Obviously, any learning program should be able to demonstrate that, but it is all the more critical when the program requires self-direction and learner-centered actions. As a result, all design and development decisions must take into account the impact they may have on learner motivation. Throughout the design and development process, the first question should always be "How may this affect the target audience's motivation to use the training program?"

The next issue to address is whether learners perceive that they will be rewarded for better performance. Although compensation structures and other reward programs typically fall out of the domain of the training department, they do affect workers' perceptions of training and how they respond to it. Thus, the way the organization rewards individuals is likely to influence the success of any training effort. It is possible for a training and development group to design and implement an excellent training program that fails not because of the quality of the training materials but because of users' beliefs that performance improvement is not rewarded in the organization. Because of this possibility, it is important to assess the perceived relationship between performance improvement and rewards in your company. (See question 3 in Survey 3.1 on page 36 for an example of how to assess this relationship.)

Finally, if employees do not value the rewards they receive for better performance, then those rewards are not likely to motivate them to learn how to perform better. (Question 4 in Survey 3.1 assesses this belief.)

Define and Communicate Goals

Goals may also enhance user motivation (Baron and Byrne, 1994; Locke and Latham, 1990). Because every effort should be made to develop WBT that learners perceive to be helpful in reaching their performance goals, part of the assessment phase (discussed in detail in chapter 5) will incorporate defining those goals for the various target audiences. It also will involve identifying the performance goals that the organization and upper management value and determining how best to encourage learner acceptance of those goals. In assessing the performance goals, consider what impact WBT may have on individuals' beliefs about their abilities to reach those goals (Ormrod, 1995). To encourage learners to believe they can succeed, you must clearly define the learning objectives. This will promote learner motivation and persistence because people are more likely to stay engaged in a learning effort if these conditions exist:

● The learners know what is expected of them.

● They believe that they can meet those expectations.

● They clearly understand the benefits associated with working toward the goals.

Defining clear objectives and goals enables learners to know the organization's expectations of them. Several training features can also help them determine how able they are to meet the objectives of various program components or determine how they can develop that ability. Those components

Survey 3.1. Sample instrument for measuring learner motivation.

Please circle the number that most closely reflects your reaction to each of the following statements.

Key to circled responses:

    1 SA = I strongly agree with the statement.
    2 A = I agree with the statement.
    3 N = I neither agree nor disagree with the statement.
    4 D = I disagree with the statement.
    5 SD = I strongly disagree with the statement.

1. Online training can help me improve my job skills and grow professionally.

1	2	3	4	5
SA	A	N	D	SD

2. Online training is likely to include training that is highly relevant to my job.

1	2	3	4	5
SA	A	N	D	SD

3. Our organization rewards employees who develop their skills and grow professionally.

1	2	3	4	5
SA	A	N	D	SD

4. I value the rewards our organization offers to employees who develop their skills and grow professionally.

1	2	3	4	5
SA	A	N	D	SD

5. I am likely to use online training.

1	2	3	4	5
SA	A	N	D	SD

Comments (e.g., how could online training be developed to support your professional development and growth most fully?):

_____

_____

_____

_____

include self assessments, tracking components, and other features that identify which parts of the program address which specific strengths and weaknesses. Those components also increase accountability for completing training tasks and enhance learners' understanding of what they are expected to accomplish in the program. For example, one tracking feature is a progress report that informs users of what they have completed and what still remains to be done in the program. As part of that feature, the organization could recognize learners as they complete certain components or phases of the training. A user could be "certified" in a particular company program and perhaps receive a certification bonus. Such features would help trainees understand the benefits associated with reaching the goals of the program.

Evaluate Perceptions

It is also important to evaluate the impact that users' general perceptions of the learning and assessment experience have on their attitudes about WBT (see Practical Tip 3.1). Here are some issues on which the evaluation should focus:

● how users feel about learning in a somewhat impersonal learning environment

● how users believe the site could facilitate personal interaction when desired or appropriate

● how users may respond to online evaluation and assessment results and how the presentation of such material can promote and encourage rather than stifle further attempts at development

● other emotional reactions that users have to WBT and its content (for example, do users see the content as useful to their development, or are they

---

Practical Tips

3.1 Managing Motivation

● Assess whether users perceive that the WBT program can help them improve their performance.
● Ask if they believe they will receive recognition and be rewarded in ways that they value for improving their performance.
● Determine what you may need to do to change perceptions about WBT and its relationship to rewards in the organization.
● Define the objectives of the training and what is expected of the learner.

frustrated by what they perceive as irrelevant materials they are required to learn to satisfy some corporate mandate?)

Corporate Culture and Attitudes toward Training and Professional Development

The success of a WBT program will also depend on current perceptions of training and development within your organization. If those attitudes are negative, implementing a new training approach using the Web may offer an opportunity to redefine those attitudes. How successfully you accomplish that redefinition will, of course, depend greatly on how successfully the Web site meets the perceived needs of the training audience.

WBT's benefits to the organization must be balanced with the impact that changes in a familiar training program may have on users. For example, if users already are comfortable using technology on the job, if they depend on e-mail for communications or document exchange, or if they use online resources as a normal part of their day, then the transition from classroom-based to Web-based learning may not be seen as a significant change. To assess your potential users' familiarity and comfort with using online resources, use Survey 3.2.

To understand the impact that attitudes toward training and training events can have on learner motivation, consider this story:

> For many years, the field personnel of a large corporation who lived throughout the United States were flown to California each January for a two-week training program that focused on updating pricing, incentive programs, and technical changes to the products. The training and development group believed that the nature of the information (for example, pricing and technical information) could be adapted easily for online learning, and they designed and implemented a training program. User testing showed that the presentation of the materials and the navigation throughout the course greatly promoted learning. Learners favorably rated all aspects of the course. When the online course was released for the use of the field staff, however, the response was uniformly negative—and that surprised and confused the training and development group. They surveyed the field personnel and found that personnel actually thought the online course was fine but they were upset about the company having eliminated their paid "vacation" with colleagues each winter.

That story illustrates a likely response to a popular training event that is moved to the Web. Trainees' reactions to and use of an online course and its

Survey 3.2. Assessing the use of online and computer resources.

Section One

Please check the box that most accurately reflects your use of the following online resources:

Online Resource	Practically Every Day	A Few Times Each Week	A Few Times Each Month	Practically Never
Electronic mail (e-mail)				
Internet				
Company's intranet				
CD-ROMs				
Plug-ins (programs used to run multimedia on the Web)				
Electronic spreadsheet programs (e.g., Excel)				
Electronic word-processing programs (e.g., MS Word, Word-Perfect)				
Other computer programs _____ _____				

Section Two

Please circle the number that most closely reflects your response to each of the following statements.

Key to circled responses:

   1 SA   =   I strongly agree with the statement.
   2 A   =   I agree with the statement.
   3 N   =   I neither agree nor disagree with the statement.
   4 D   =   I disagree with the statement.
   5 SD   =   I strongly disagree with the statement.

1. I feel comfortable using a computer.

1	2	3	4	5
SA	A	N	D	SD

continued on page 40

Survey, *continued*

2. I feel comfortable using the Internet.

1	2	3	4	5
SA	A	N	D	SD

3. I feel comfortable downloading plug-ins and other online resources that are needed to run online multimedia programs.

1	2	3	4	5
SA	A	N	D	SD

4. I feel comfortable using online resources.

1	2	3	4	5
SA	A	N	D	SD

Comments (e.g., how comfortable do you feel you would be using online training resources?):

_____

_____

_____

_____

resources will depend on a number of factors beyond design and function (see Practical Tips 3.2 and 3.3). Even if your development team has created an excellent learning resource, the initial response may be negative unless during the assessment phase, your organization identifies and does something to compensate employees for any perceived loss they experience in the transition.

Course Design Strategies

WBT challenges many long-held assumptions about training and course design because of the nature of the medium. How does one design courses that motivate and engage learners in environments that involve little or no interaction between the learner and an instructor or among several learners? Many course design issues are relevant to traditional computer-based training approaches, but the Web enables learners to access huge arrays of training options and requires them to be more self-directed than did earlier approaches. As a result, WBT requires a learner-centered approach to design and development. In chapter 5, we will discuss this approach in greater detail. For now, be aware that the need to motivate and engage learners in new ways greatly affects the design and development of training resources offered via the Web.

Constraints Imposed by Hardware and Software

Consider the following two situations.

Example 1: A Web technology group was hosting a large-scale experiment in sending a synchronous class in dairy science via the Internet to more than 300 dairy farmers and agricultural extension

---

Practical Tips

3.2 Assessing the Impact of Offering Web-Based Content

● Use interviews and other survey methods to determine how course changes from a classroom-based to an online format might affect participation and learner motivation.
● Assess whether hands-on demonstrations and participation are critical to learning the materials. (If so, a Web-based approach may not be effective.)
● If the course is currently very popular or unpopular, assess how converting the course to an online learning experience may affect its popularity.

Practical Tips

3.3 Unique Considerations for WBT Managers

● How can my development team assess and respond to the potential psychological impact of WBT on those using our training programs?
● What are the current attitudes in the organization toward training?
● What are the current attitudes about the use of online resources?
● What hardware and software issues may affect the design and implementation of WBT in my organization?

agents in five states. Twelve universities were collaborating on the project. Although some of the technical issues had been resolved, several either had been ignored or had not been anticipated. For example, many of the students could not get their browsers to work. Some of the farmers had telephone lines that had been installed in the 1930s and couldn't handle Net traffic. The students were using a variety of Internet service providers, some of which were incompatible with the training format. There were other problems ranging from bad internal voice modems to bizarre computer configurations. As a result, the training scheduled to start at the end of January was delayed until the beginning of March.

Example 2: Field personnel in a large health services organization were using laptop computers with 386 microprocessor chips when the training and development department implemented an online performance support program intended to link employees more effectively to learning resources using the company's intranet. Although Windows 95 had been available for several years, the organization was committed to a Windows 3.1 standard. The training and development department worked with an external vendor to develop the programming code for the learning system, but the vendor assumed that the company was using Windows 95 and developed the software to function within that operating system. At the time of deployment, the online program simply did not run on a Windows 3.1 operating system. Although the programmers were able to develop a solution, the final implementation of the online program was delayed several weeks.

Those two examples suggest some of the problems that may arise when training managers do not understand the technical environment of their organizations.

Traditional training approaches are much less dependent on a company's hardware and software than are Web-based programs. Now it is critical that training managers understand the basic technical details about an organization's computer and network infrastructure. This means knowing about the operating systems, the Web browsers in use, the computer equipment's hardware specifications, and the network capacity. In chapter 4, we will discuss these technological issues.

Chapter 4. Technology Considerations

Developers of WBT often have state-of-the-art hardware, the most recent browsers and operating systems, and other high-end and expensive equipment, but you cannot assume your users will possess this same level of functional sophistication. If you are managing the development of an online learning resource, you must consider the constraints placed on the end product by the users' equipment and software. Failure to consider those essential ingredients can greatly affect the functionality and appearance of a WBT site. The following scenario illustrates this reality.

> A training and development group had a limited budget with which to create an online resource. In a month's time they developed a two-hour Web-based tutorial that included a thorough review of the resource using the equipment on which it was created. To control costs, the group decided to eliminate what they thought were unnecessary development steps, one of which was user testing. At implementation, the training and development staff were perplexed to find that users were taking an average of seven hours over periods of up to two weeks to complete the tutorial. When they investigated the cause of the delays, they were told by users that the text appeared on screen as fluorescent yellow on a green background and that the users simply could not bear to look at it for extended periods of time. The developers' machines had screens that used millions of colors and the text had been highly readable, but the users had lower-end laptops with 16-color screens. As a result, 20,000 users spent an additional five hours to complete the two-hour tutorial. Had the developers tested the program with learners using their own computers, the developers would have seen the impact of the color shift on legibility and could have redesigned the course to save roughly 100,000 hours of time (12,500 staff days).

Although the "palette shift" described there is less likely to occur today because of improvements in browser software, the point remains the same: overlooking users' equipment can be one of the costliest missteps in developing a WBT program.

Technological Variables

To avoid problems similar to the one described above, it is critical that you discuss technology issues with the programmers and other production staff, and come to complete agreement about the hardware and software configurations to which the system should be built. Below is a detailed discussion of the end-user technological variables that can significantly affect WBT. Practical Tip 4.1 addresses technology matters from the manager's perspective, and Checklist 4.1 presents end-user variables and asks critical questions to help you assess the status of those variables in your organization.

Connection Speed (Bandwidth)

The connection speed affects how rapidly the user receives data from the WBT program. The more complex the online resources (for example, video and other media that would require a plug-in), the higher the bandwidth needed to ensure the quality and speed of the transmission. Many organizations have T1 or better telephone lines that greatly facilitate the speed of transmission (except when delays occur as the result of a high volume of Internet traffic). Many field staff, however, access a company's intranet using modems that vary from 14.4 kbps to 56.6 kbps. Downloading large files over a 14.4 kbps modem is tedious and may cause users to lose interest

---

Practical Tips

4.1 Technology Issues for Managers

● How can my development team assess, design, and develop training that is consistent with the hardware and software currently in use (or that will be in use at the time of deployment)?
  ○ How do the operating systems and browsers in use affect the design and development of the training site?
  ○ How might the connection speeds available to trainees affect the types of media that can be used?
  ○ What types of plug-ins or extensions am I willing to require users to download?
  ○ What type of database will be required to support the features and benefits desired?
● What is my working relationship with the IT department? If it is currently challenging, what can I do to improve that relationship?

in a WBT program. In general, text files transfer quickly even over slower modems, but such files lack the higher-end capabilities of the Web for video and audio presentations.

Checklist 4.1. Review and assessment of hardware and software issues.

Issue	Sample Assessment Questions
• Connection speed (bandwidth) (e.g., 14.4 kbps, 56.6 kbps; modems; T1 [trunk] lines)	• How connected are users? • Do users access the site directly via the company intranet? Via a T1 line or slower-speed modems (14.4 kbps)? • Are there other connection issues (e.g., size of files that will be transmitted)?
• Type of microprocessing chip and speed (e.g., 486, Pentium 2, 166 MHz, 266 MHz)	• Do users have older equipment with slower chips?
• Random access memory (e.g., 4 MB, 64 MB)	• Do the majority of users have 16 MB of RAM or greater?
• Browsers (e.g., Netscape, Internet Explorer)	• Has the company standardized on a particular browser and version number (e.g., Netscape 4.0)?
• Plug-ins and extensions (e.g., Shockwave, RealAudio)	• Which plug-ins do most users have?
• Monitor resolution and color depth (e.g., 640 × 480, 16 color, 32 bit)	• What types of monitors are in use?
• Database (if applicable) (e.g., Oracle, Sybase)	• What database application will be used, and is there in-house expertise with that database?
• Hosting issues (e.g., maintenance of server on which the site resides)	• Will the IT department host the training site, or will an outside vendor host it?
• Security concerns (e.g., firewalls, cookies)	• Does additional security need to be created to protect the site?
• Sound card (e.g., 8 bit, 16 bit)	• What sound cards are in use?
• Video accelerator card and VRAM (e.g., 4 MB)	• What video accelerator cards are in use?
• Operating systems (e.g., Windows 3.1, Mac OS, Windows 95)	• What operating systems are in use? • Has the company standardized on a particular operating system?

Bandwidth issues can strongly influence design and development issues. In many cases, developers target the lowest common denominator for access when developing WBT because of the wide variation in connection speeds. Such targeting can mean that the Web site is limited in its use of sophisticated media such as video and interactive exercises. Many Web sites with fancy graphics have been released but not used either because they could not be downloaded or because the downloads took longer than users were willing to wait.

Random Access Memory and Processor Type and Speed

In addition to the online connection speed, the amount of random access memory and the type of chip in the computer will affect the speed of transmission and the presentation of data. Users with eight megabytes of RAM and a 66-megahertz chip or less are likely to encounter slower transmissions of data or become frustrated if large files must be downloaded to use the WBT program.

Browsers

Browsers are Internet applications that provide access to online resources; Netscape and Internet Explorer are two examples of browser types. Each browser software program has multiple versions that result from the repeated updates required to accommodate the ever-changing capabilities of the Web. Because of these updates, the employees in your organization may be using different versions of a particular browser or may even be using different browser programs. Higher-end Web options, such as the latest video and audio capabilities, require the latest browser versions as well as higher bandwidth and certain plug-ins. Users with older versions may not be able to access some components of the training program (see Figure 4.1). If it is appropriate, the training manager and production team may decide to build their training program to suit a specific version of a particular browser and then encourage trainees or the IT department to download and use only that software.

At an earlier time in the Web's history, users had to pay for browser software and upgrades. Establishing a minimum standard, therefore, would have required users to purchase the software or an upgrade. Now, however, most browsers are free and can be downloaded or upgraded immediately from the browser producer's Web site.

Plug-Ins and Extensions

Many programs used in developing WBT programs require users to have or to download specific plug-ins or extensions. In rare cases, the plug-ins are not compatible across platforms (that is, they won't work on both a PC and a Macintosh system) or are not available for certain platforms. As a result, multimedia components may have to be restricted to those programs that use plug-ins and extensions readily available to the learner population. Some of the more popular plug-ins include Macromedia's Shockwave, RealAudio, RealVideo, and Adobe Acrobat Reader. Those and several other popular plug-ins are listed in Table 4.1, and Online Exercise 4 on page 53 helps you download and install plug-ins from the Web.

Monitor Resolution

The types of monitors in use in your organization can affect the appearance of the online resources significantly. Screens that are visually appealing and highly readable on a monitor that offers millions of colors may be unappealing and difficult to read on a monitor that offers 16 colors (older laptops) or even 256 colors. Again, design and development activities and user testing should take into consideration and determine the effects of the different monitors in use.

Databases

Some type of database program will be needed to store your training Web site and give access to training materials, user records, and statistics. Available database software varies in size and power. Oracle, Sybase, and Informix products are enterprise-level databases typically used in corporate and other large-scale networked systems. Microsoft Access, for example, is a limited-scale database environment that can be used in a smaller network. The size and power of the database used in either a customized or a commercial training system will influence the design and development of the training program. Smaller database environments will limit the amount of information that can be stored and the speed at which it can be accessed.

Figure 4.1

This screen presents the type of message that a learner might receive when the multimedia image at the site requires a newer browser version than the learner has.

Table 4.1. Popular computer plug-ins.

Plug-In (Vendor)	Function	URL
● Acrobat Reader (Adobe)	Allows one to use files saved in portable document format. PDF allows users on various platforms (e.g., PCs, Macs) to download the file. PDF is widely used on the Internet.	www.adobe.com/ prodindex/acrobat/ readstep.html
● CMX Viewer (Corel)	Displays high-resolution graphic files.	www.corel.com/ corelcmx/INDEX.HTM
● Envoy (Tumbleweed)	Displays documents on the Internet exactly as they were designed.	www/twcorp.com/ plugin.htm
● Formula One/NET (Visual Components)	Displays spreadsheets that are compatible with Excel and can include links (URLs) to other Web resources.	www.logon-int.com/ Tools_1/html/web_ development_tools_ 22.html
● Neuron (Asymetrix)	Plays animations and programs developed using ToolBook II.	www.asymetrix.com/ products/toolbook2/ neuron/
● RealAudio (Progressive Networks)	Plays live, real-time, and other audio files.	www.realaudio.com/
● RealVideo (Progressive Networks)	Plays live, real-time, and other video files.	www.realaudio.com/
● RealPlayer (Progressive Networks)	Plays RealAudio and RealVideo files.	www.realaudio.com/
● Shockwave (Macromedia)	Plays files that were developed using Authorware and Director.	http://special. macromedia.com/ pointcse/sw1.html
● ToolVox (Voxware)	Plays high-quality audio files.	www.voxware.com/
● Vivoplay	Plays streaming video files.	www.vivo.com/ dload.htm
● VR Scout VRML, Pueblo (Chaco Communications)	Plays VRML (virtual reality) files.	www.chaco.com/ vrscout/
● Worldview (Platinum)	Plays VRML files.	www.intervista.com/

Developing a customized database for use on the Web demands programming expertise. The programmers must design the software to fit the system and to ensure robust (that is, stable and accurate) processing of the data. They also will need to develop a coded CGI application to initiate and maintain the query and storage conversations that must be established between the database engine and the Web server with which the user's machine communicates. (CGI programming enables messages from a user's client machine and the server machine to interact.)

As a manager of Web-based training and development interventions, you do not have to understand the specifics of database programming, particularly if you choose a commercial training system. But because the success of the program depends on the ability of the software to support what the training site offers, it is critical that you have an excellent working relationship with the programmers developing your training database. If you plan to choose a commercial training system, consult with someone who can evaluate the power and robustness of the system's database.

Hosting Issues

A training Web site must reside on a server that can be accessed via the Web or via your company's intranet. A number of vendors offer Web site hosting services that include support and maintenance. The first step in selecting a host for your WBT program is to determine what resources are available (see Practical Tip 4.2). If your organization's IT department has a large budget and the latest technology, it most likely will be able to host the site and provide the necessary support and maintenance. In smaller organizations, an external hosting agreement may be the best approach because it does not demand the capital expenditures required to obtain, maintain, and update hosting technology.

Security: Firewalls

Network security is primarily intended to protect a network from outsiders who might intentionally or unintentionally compromise or damage network resources. Most organizations have intranets that are protected by a "firewall" that denies access to those who lack authorization. In most cases, an organization's IT personnel will have worked with an internal or external security consultant to establish the protective system. Your primary concern will be to ensure that each member of the intended training audience has access to the site.

If trainees connect to the WBT program both via the company intranet and from mobile locations, the IT department may need to develop a "cookie" that authorizes use of the system when users sign in, and then tracks their progress. Basically, a cookie is an electronic calling card that enables the server to recognize the identity and history of a user. The cookie, therefore, can be used as an authorization application and as a mechanism for tracking a learner's use of the resource. For example, if a learner only accessed a portion of an online learning resource in a previous session, the server can be set up to recognize this and start the learner at the appropriate place. The cookie does not have to be part of a security application.

Sound and Video Accelerator Cards

Sound and video cards allow a computer to run video and audio applications. Cards in use may impose restrictions on the types of video and audio programming that can be used in the WBT program. For example, highly interactive interventions may not run on slower accelerator cards. The visual design personnel who craft your training Web site will have to consider all of the organization's computer hardware and software configurations, including all sound and video cards in use.

Operating Systems

Within an organization, learners may be using diverse operating systems, including Windows 95, Windows 98, Windows NT, a version of the Mac OS, UNIX, and others. The functionality of a WBT program may be limited by

---

Practical Tips

4.2 Hosting Arrangements

● Determine whether your organization has a network in place that could host the training site.

● Determine whether you can rely on active support from the IT department.

● Assess your organization's financial and technical resources to provide the technology needed to support the site.

● Consider the time frames associated with the training program and determine whether there is sufficient time to support, buy (or lease), and develop the necessary technology.

● Assess whether it might be best to have everyone use an Internet service provider (ISP) to access the site (an external hosting arrangement could be supported through the use of an ISP).

If part of the hosting solution involves learners' using an ISP, examine the service provider's support of various platforms, remote access options, bandwidth, reliability, development and support services, and such other services as e-mail and server maintenance.

the operating systems in use. For example, a program designed for Windows 98 may not have full functionality if the learner is using an earlier version of Windows. If learners in an organization use different operating systems and platforms (for example, PCs and Macintoshes), program design may need to accommodate cross-platform use. User testing should include people who are working on each of the various operating systems and platforms.

If your organization uses a variety of operating systems (for example, from Windows 3.1 to Windows NT), it may be necessary to decide what minimum operating system will be required to use the full capabilities of your online resources. Making that decision means that users of operating systems below the minimum standard either will have to upgrade or forfeit their use of parts or all of the learning program.

Size and Functionality

It is necessary to have a Web site (identified by a specific uniform resource locator, or URL) as a place where relevant information can be accessed and stored. Sites themselves will vary considerably in terms of composition and complexity. As a training manager, you must ensure that how you expect the Web site to function is actually reflected on the screen. For example, a Web site composed primarily of text and simple graphic files with no interactive features may be appropriate for presenting content related to a specific topic or a single lesson. It may be possible to implement a simple WBT site using an off-the-shelf site development tool or writing a simple hypertext markup language (HTML) program, but if a full course offered via the Web is planned or if the course will feature audio and video components, you must create a Web site that can accommodate these various components.

If any interactivity is part of the overall course design—that is, if learners will be expected to complete practical learning exercises online as part of the course activities—you will need to include CGI programming in the development. If animations are included to illustrate specific points of a lesson, you must include more complex programming, such as plug-ins, extensions, and server tools, along with appropriate software licensing. Finally, the more complex the site becomes, the more staffing and financial resources you will need. In subsequent chapters of this book, we will discuss the specific staffing needs demanded by the features and benefits you select for your training Web site.

The Ideal Situation

In the best case, every learner has access to a T1 line (or better), the latest versions of browser software, and state-of-the-art hardware. That may be the situation in organizations that strongly support technology and maintain high standards for the technology in use. If so, potential technological constraints will be less of an issue in WBT development. But such circumstances will be the exception instead of the rule. Because the hardware and software throughout many organizations varies dramatically, the design, implementation, and management of most WBT programs will have to address hardware and software limitations. Where both older and newer technology are in use, the program may be set up to offer both video and nonvideo as well as framed and nonframed versions. A framed Web page has sections that are able to move independently of each other; for example, there may be a table of contents on the left-hand side and a scrolling contents section on the right-hand side of the Web page.

The Sum of the Parts

In many cases, the technological issues that affect the creation of WBT and development intervention combine in unpredictable ways. Truly, the whole may be greater than the sum of its parts. Even when each of the technology concerns presented in this chapter is evaluated, situations may arise that call for flexibility and modifications to existing designs and schedules. To the degree possible, your development team will want to eliminate such outcomes, but be certain to allow for the unexpected to occur and for response times to be accommodated in the schedule.

Online Exercise 4. Plug-ins.

● The following exercise gives you an opportunity to assess your level of comfort with plug-ins. From a user's perspective, downloading and installing of a plug-in is one of the most common requirements for use of a particular site or Web component. This exercise gives you an opportunity to download a plug-in to run a particular application. WBT programs that make use of streaming audio or video or of other multimedia components are likely to require plug-ins.

Step 1

Open your browser (for example, Netscape, Internet Explorer).

Step 2

Go to one of the following (select one that requires downloading a plug-in that you believe you do NOT currently have on your computer):

- ● http:/www.starcreations.com/gamedowner/ga-shock.htm (a collection of Shockwave games)
- ● http:/www.amazon.com (enter the name of your favorite group and play a track, if available; this requires the RealAudio plug-in)

Step 3

Choose a program and try to run it. If you already have the plug-in, you will be able to view the video/audio. But if you do not have the appropriate plug-in, your browser will let you know that you need to download it. Follow the directions to do so.

Step 4

Play the game or view the video/audio (depending on the site).

Questions

- ● Did you have any difficulties downloading the plug-in?
- ● Did you have any difficulties with the video/audio once you had downloaded the plug-in?
- ● How does your knowledge of this process compare with that of the average user of your planned WBT program?
- ● How might the need to download a plug-in affect use of that aspect of the training program?

SECTION TWO

Managing the Development and Design of Web-Based Training

Chapter 5. Designing and Developing Learning Interventions

The nature of a WBT program can range from a simple, relatively inexpensive e-mail course to a customized system developed and programmed specifically for an organization. This chapter is particularly relevant if your organization plans to develop its own WBT system or to customize a commercial training system. Even if you decide to adopt a turnkey training system that allows for very little customization, understanding the entire development process will help you select and manage the system that best meets your training needs (see Practical Tip 5.1).

Traditional Versus Learner-Centered Instructional Approaches

As noted earlier, WBT challenges many long-held assumptions about training. Traditionally, learning is developed from the trainers' point of view. Teachers decide *for the learner* what is required from outside by defining

---

Practical Tips

5.1 Primary Management Issues

These questions are of paramount importance in managing a training program on the Web:

- How can I guide my team in its design and development of the site in order to create a successful training program?
- What aspects of each phase of the design, development, implementation, and maintenance process require special attention?

Use the Project Management Checklist and Planner (Checklist 5.1) to help you answer these questions and evaluate the project's progress continually.

characteristics of instruction, curriculum, assessment, and management to achieve a desired learning outcome. In recent years, however, trainers have begun collaborating with learners to enhance each learner's experience by examining the learner's unique talents, capabilities, and experiences to develop appropriate training. The developing success of these collaborative efforts to learning has led to instructional approaches that engage learners as active participants. One example of this newer approach is "just-in-time, just-for-me" learning.

WBT systems are poised to play a key role in this evolution in theory and practice of how training supports the needs of individuals and work teams. In many ways, Web-based learning is an extension of distance learning, which originated in response to geographic constraints. It focuses on designing and implementing interactive instructional programming for two or more people at two or more locations, separated by location or in time (Wagner, 1994). Web-based learning systems also overcome geographic constraints, but they operate with a different focus: they offer users seamless access to informational resources and provide trainees with strategies, tactics, and tools for creating personalized instructional programs. Distance education models emphasize overcoming physical distance without requiring a rethinking of the basic concept of "training," but WBT, as a medium, encourages a radical revision of the goals and philosophy of training by focusing on an individual's ability to access information and instructional opportunities without regard to physical location.

Learner-Centered Principles and What Training Managers Need to Know

A great deal of research has studied an approach to training that focuses on the learner (a learner-centered approach). Many trainers may not be interested in the underlying theory and research, but it is useful to understand the implications of that research. A basic summary of the findings in the form of learner-centered principles is presented in Practical Tip 5.2 (American Psychological Association, 1993; McCombs, 1992). An awareness of those principles will help you create a more successful WBT program.

Essentially, the learning principles translate to the following statement: People learn as individuals on thebases of their past experiences, social status, and cultural factors as well as on their levels of self-esteem and confidence.

The core truth of a learner-centered approach is that what works for one person may or may not work for another. A learning program that ignores those principles is less likely to be effective, particularly for people who feel alienated or who see formal learning as either irrelevant or threatening.

Practical Tips

5.2 Principles of Learner-Centered Instruction

● **Principle 1: Learning does not occur in a vacuum.** Learners discover and construct meaning from information and experience based on their unique perceptions, thoughts, and feelings.

● **Principle 2: More information does not necessarily mean more learning.** Learners try to create meaningful uses for knowledge, regardless of the quantity and quality of the information presented.

● **Principle 3: Learners link new knowledge to existing information in ways that make sense to them.** Recalling new knowledge is facilitated when it can be tied to a learner's current knowledge.

● **Principle 4: Personality influences learning.** Learners have varying degrees of self-confidence and they differ in the clarity of their personal goals and expectations for success and failure.

● **Principle 5: Learners want to learn.** People are naturally curious and they enjoy learning, but personal insecurity and fear of failure often get in the way.

● **Principle 6: Learners like challenges.** Learners are most creative when learning is challenging and meets their individual needs.

● **Principle 7: Learners are individuals.** Not all learners are at the same stage of physical, intellectual, emotional, and social development, and they differ in their cultural backgrounds. Although the basic principles of learning apply to all learners, regardless of those differences, trainers must take into account such differences among learners.

● **Principle 8: The learning environment is important.** People learn best in a friendly, socially interactive, and diverse environment.

● **Principle 9: Learners like positive reinforcement.** Learning environments that support the self-esteem and respect of the trainee tend to be more successful.

● **Principle 10: Past experience matters.** Personal beliefs and impressions from earlier learning experiences color learners' worldviews and their approaches to learning.

Note: Interest in establishing clear guidelines for designing and developing learner-centered instructions and training has resulted in much activity during the past decade (e.g., McCombs, King, and Wagner, 1993; Wagner and McCombs, 1995). The principles of learner-centered instruction build on previous research and development work (motivated by school-reform efforts) to demonstrate their relevancy for individuals working in corporate training and professional development settings.

Choosing Appropriate Course Content and Form

Identifying appropriate learning materials for online delivery is one of the most difficult challenges facing a training manager. Most trainers find it easier to develop content to test knowledge of demonstrable tasks than of other tasks (see Exercise 5.1 to understand how the nature of tasks can differ). But rapid developments in Web technologies open a new menu of possibilities for delivering content. (To see how many of these components are now being used, refer to the sites indicated in the online exercise in chapter 9.)

Interactivity and the Choice of a Web-Based Training System

The quality of a training Web site will depend on several factors, but quality is most often defined by the interactivity offered. Interaction—or the perception of it—generally increases learners' ratings of the WBT quality. Many

---

Exercise 5.1. Understanding the nature of the course content.

The purpose of this exercise is to illustrate how the nature of the knowledge or skills to be taught affects the ease with which it can be taught via the Web.

Skills to be taught are either *demonstrable* or *judgmental* in nature (Laughlin and Ellis, 1986). Both skill types can be taught online, but it is generally easier to develop training for and assess the impact of demonstrable knowledge. WBT that focuses on "soft skills" (judgmental skills) development is likely to require more time to create and often demands that SMEs come to consensus about what is the best way to improve performance in a particular soft skill. Also, be aware that learners are more likely to want to discuss training associated with a judgmental task than with a demonstrable task. As a result, interactivity is often a critical component of judgmental or soft skills training and must be incorporated in the design of the program.

Perform the following two exercises to learn how demonstrable and judgmental tasks differ. That will help you identify the nature of the task performance your organization needs to improve.

A Demonstrable Task

Mary Lou Jackson bought a house in 1985 for X dollars. In 1995, she sold the house for 25 percent more than she paid for it. Mary Lou must pay in taxes 50 percent of her gain on the house. How much must she pay in taxes?

a. 0.25X   b. 0.10X   c. X/8   d. X/16   e. 0.15X

training specialists believe that interaction is the most important WBT component (Wagner, 1997, 1998). For example, users typically judge a video conference as a better learning experience than a conference call. As a result, Web-based systems using streaming video or audio files are likely to be perceived as better than those relying solely on text. The development and construction of such systems will probably be influenced both by budget limitations and by hardware/software considerations. In choosing either customized development or a commercial training system, consider both current capabilities and your organization's future commitment to technology.

The quality of video transmissions via the Internet has improved dramatically in the past several years. In general, WBT programs are enhanced when high-quality, interactive presentations are available (for example, video, online lectures). Thus, even if the current course content does not include online lectures, a training and development team may design the learning environment so that these types of courses can be offered in the future. As part of the evaluation of commercial training systems, determine how well the system handles these online presentations.

The task is demonstrable in that, if you know the correct answer, you can demonstrate it easily to another person as follows:

> Let's say Mary Lou paid $100,000 dollars (the X value) for the house. In 1995, she sold the house for 25 percent more than the purchase price, or $125,000. The gain on the house was $25,000. She must pay 50 percent of the gain or $12,500 ($25,000 × 0.5). The original amount (X) was $100,000. The tax of $12,500 is one-eighth of $100,000. Therefore, the amount of the tax is X/8 (answer [c]).

Any task for which there is one or few correct solutions, such as properly attaching a component to a machine, using a word-processing system to merge names and addresses to a letter, or mixing two chemicals for a production process, is an example of a demonstrable task.

A Judgmental Task

> Discuss with a colleague and write a statement of your beliefs about how negative feedback should be given to employees and whether it is likely to motivate them to improve their performance.

That task is judgmental because the correct answer is more difficult to demonstrate and more open to dispute. In other words, the correct answer depends on a person's judgment of the information provided. For example, you might have a theory that supports your answer, but others could say that in their experience, your theory does not work. Soft skills, such as coaching, managing meetings, and so forth, are examples of judgmental tasks.

Online Exercises 5A, 5B, and 5C, beginning on page 74, address various aspects of interactivity.

Budget

As you make decisions about how to develop and implement a Web-based training system, you may have to take budgetary considerations into account. You may not be able to do everything you had envisioned. However, a limited budget does not necessarily mean that you have to settle for an inferior WBT program. You can still take advantage of many key benefits of the Web: online communication with instructors and other learners via e-mail, chat rooms, and message boards; access to the vast resources of the Internet; and learner-centered design. In fact, some WBT designers have found cases in which low-budget alternatives are more effective and engaging than expensive options (for example, a streaming video on how to build a cell phone may be less effective than a series of relatively simple still photo with clickable elements) (Fister, 1998).

Goals and Objectives

Ultimately, the system selected or developed and the components that it comprises will depend on specific company goals and objectives. For example, if the goal is only to update knowledge about pricing information, then interactive exercises, a full resource library, and other sophisticated components may not be necessary. On the other hand, if the goal is to offer a complete sales approach and methodology, then interactive exercises and an extensive library are likely to be parts of your site.

Alpha to Omega: From Assessment to Ongoing Maintenance

The remainder of this chapter will look at each step in designing and developing a WBT program, and it will describe both the standard and the unique issues involved in creating such a program. Understanding that process will help you manage the training project overall. The flowchart in Figure 5.1 depicts the alpha-to-omega model and its major facets.

The alpha-to-omega model presented here is similar to those used to define the development process for distance education and other traditional approaches to learning. If you have a background in or an understanding of instructional design, you are likely to be familiar with the process stages that guide the development of a WBT program. Within each phase of Web-based development, however, there are activities that may be new or technology specific. There are six phases in the model:

1. assessment
2. design
3. development
4. implementation
5. evaluation
6. maintenance

Figure 5.1. Alpha to omega: WBT from assessment to maintenance.

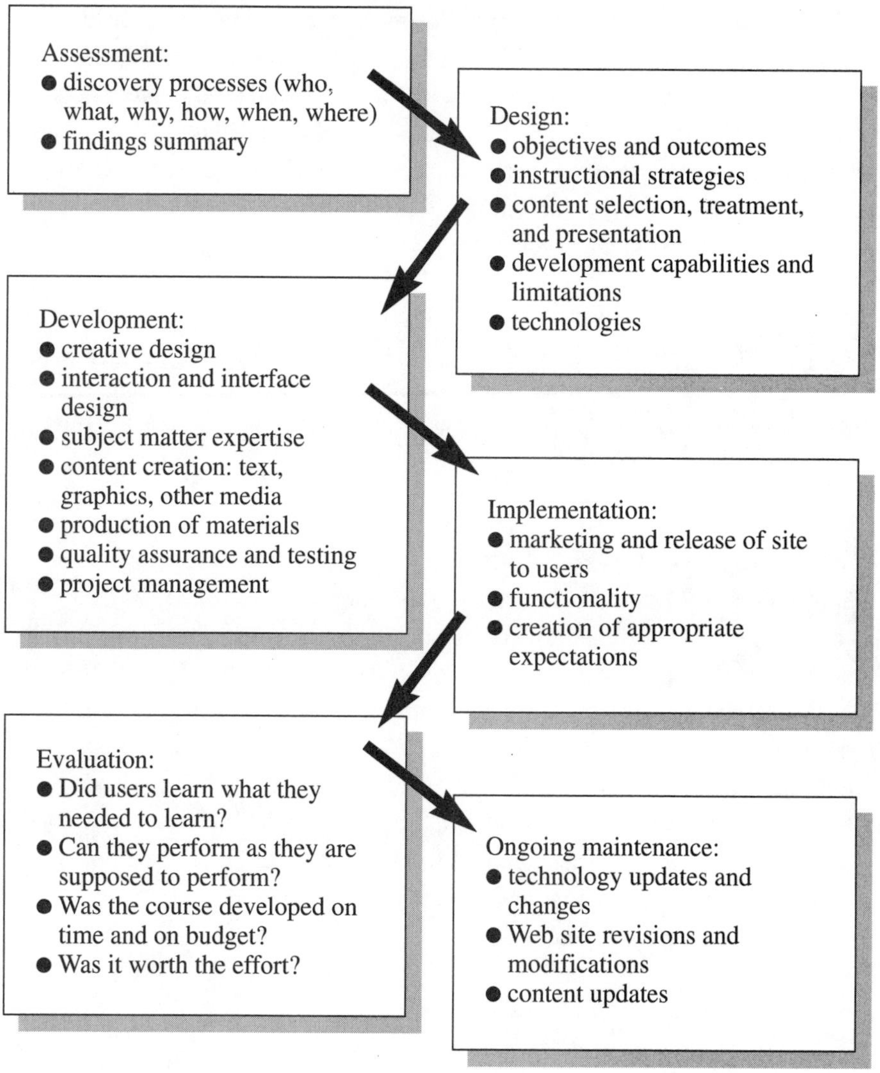

Assessment:
- discovery processes (who, what, why, how, when, where)
- findings summary

Design:
- objectives and outcomes
- instructional strategies
- content selection, treatment, and presentation
- development capabilities and limitations
- technologies

Development:
- creative design
- interaction and interface design
- subject matter expertise
- content creation: text, graphics, other media
- production of materials
- quality assurance and testing
- project management

Implementation:
- marketing and release of site to users
- functionality
- creation of appropriate expectations

Evaluation:
- Did users learn what they needed to learn?
- Can they perform as they are supposed to perform?
- Was the course developed on time and on budget?
- Was it worth the effort?

Ongoing maintenance:
- technology updates and changes
- Web site revisions and modifications
- content updates

Assessment

Assessment encompasses a range of activities used to determine how learning and support experiences should be developed. Among other things, it considers the type and quality of performance that is expected when learning has been completed and it targets the essential tasks that need to be addressed as the learning experience is constructed. Assessment also examines the domain of the content to be included in a course or a program of individual study. That ensures that the information needed to cover a topic adequately is actually considered in content selection decisions. It also may help define the level and amount of content that a particular target audience needs to achieve mastery of the knowledge and skills needed to support optimal performance.

During the assessment phase, incorporate the perspectives of a broad array of stakeholders, including the learners for whom the course is intended and the managers responsible for monitoring learners' progress. Consider the expectations of experts in the field, and the nature of the marketplace in which "high-performing learners" demonstrate their skill and content mastery. Also at that time, take a close look at some of the attributes of your target audience to be certain that performance expectations and resource design elements (for example, tone and mode of presentation) are articulated appropriately. Finally, assess the context within which the learning experience is to

---

Practical Tips

5.3 Assessment Questions

To ensure that the training you are developing meets the existing needs of your organization, ask the following questions of people who can help you define outcome objectives and expectations.

- In what job categories do workers need performance improvement?
- What skill gaps or deficiencies exist for each of those job categories?
- What kinds of professional development could benefit staff members most significantly?
- What strategic goals and objectives has upper management set, and what skills are needed to accomplish those goals and objectives?
- Is training the appropriate means to eliminating the identified performance gaps or to encouraging competent performers to continue to improve their knowledge and skills?
- If training is appropriate, what types of training are most likely to meet your organization's needs?

be implemented, specify the need for technical support, and ensure that resource scheduling issues have been addressed. Practical Tip 5.3 presents questions to ask when assessing the needs of stakeholders, and Practical Tip 5.4 suggests ways to conduct your assessment.

One area that presents a broad array of challenges when developing WBT programs is the technology needed to implement the program, both hardware and software. Technology influences the overall design and the multimedia features that the Web site can offer. In most organizations, the answers to technology questions are influenced directly by the perspectives of the organization's information technology or management information systems staffs. Training and development professionals need to work closely with their organization's technology professionals to determine the impact that a proposed electronic learning design may have on technology infrastructure, services, and support. At the same time, IT staff need to be increasingly aware that a technology solution alone will not be sufficient to meet the needs of the various stakeholders who typically are involved in an enterprise-wide performance improvement effort. Assessment identifies the opportunities and barriers to potential success before one travels too far down any particular path.

Design

Training design efforts typically involve reviewing information collected during the assessment phase and constructing a proposal for meeting as many of the stakeholders' needs as is feasible, given the available resources

---

Practical Tips

5.4 Techniques for Conducting Assessment

Here are some of the ways to gather assessment information:
- observations
- analysis of existing documents
- reviews of the organization's annual reports
- surveys, questionnaires, and interviews
- literature reviews
- reviews of industry summaries
- focus groups or user-requirement workshops
- reviews of current courses, and of course and instructor evaluations
- reviews of recommendations for next steps from any previous reports that evaluated training and performance support programs

and circumstances. In constructing learning designs, whether at the enterprise level or the department level, these actions are accomplished:

- Learning resources, such as content, exercises, and tools, are identified.

- Performance standards are established.

- Performance and learning objectives are articulated.

- Primary and secondary resources for supporting the delivery of a learning experience are identified.

- Instructional strategies and tactics are specified.

- Any additional media needed to support the delivery of a learning experience are called out.

The end result of the design phase is a design document that describes in detail four key elements of the learning experience that must be in place for that experience to be successful:

1. Objectives and Outcomes

Before undertaking a learning experience, trainees must know what is expected and what they should be able to do as a result of the instructional or performance improvement intervention. State the objectives using action verbs and take into account the conditions under which an expected performance is to be offered. Write the objectives in a way that makes them measurable.

2. Learning Strategies

Learning strategies help define the approach to be used to ensure that content presentation is appropriate for achieving the intended outcomes. Examples of learning strategies include interaction techniques, learning activities, and attentional and mnemonic devices. Learning strategies also consider learning styles and cognitive strategies that learners are likely to use, so that designs can complement the natural abilities that learners bring to the tasks at hand.

3. Content Selection, Treatment, and Presentation

Addressing content selection, treatment, and presentation involves asking a number of questions:

- What needs to be said?

- How much information is enough?

- How can one tell if there is too much information for a given task?

- How should content be presented?

- If various content objects or pieces are being selected to train people to complete a task, what must be done to ensure some measure of consistency in pacing and presentation among the content pieces?

- What kind of conceptual connections are needed to provide a coherent presentation of content pieces?

- To what degree are users able to manage their own navigation among the content objects or pieces to achieve a particular learning outcome?

- Are the examples clear and relevant?

- Are the examples appropriate for all prospective members of a target audience?

4. In-House Development Capabilities and Limitations

Organizations must decide who will construct the learning resources. Is the intention to create a customized WBT program or to use off-the-shelf courseware and online training tools? If off-the-shelf courseware and tools are used, are they modular enough to be customized to the specific needs of various target audiences and other organizational demands? Will training and development staff be "replaced" by the introduction of online performance and training support, or will these online tools better enable training professionals to support the real learning needs of the organization by boosting their abilities to respond to diagnosed training needs? Will there be support for ongoing maintenance and revisions to the online learning environment?

Your key function as a WBT project manager during the design phase is to approve the design decisions and to relate them to the overall project goals and objectives. In addition, you will help the team finalize design decisions and determine the specific features and benefits that the Web site will offer.

Development

Development involves the actual production of the interventions called for in the design phase. In a setting where commercially available training materials form the foundation of the resources that will be used, development activities may represent only a small part of the endeavor. Even so, training professionals must know enough about how to develop effective interventions to be able to evaluate the quality of any off-the-shelf training product.

In general, an effective learning resource development plan needs to specify how the following activities are going to be accomplished or ensured:

- **Content creation:** The actual development of content, including revisions to existing courseware, is based on the decisions made in the design phase. The quality of the course development should rely on the standards of good instructional design and acknowledge the special characteristics of WBT (for example, just-in-time, just-for-me resources).

Information presented to learners must be developed so that they can use it effectively. That means developing content and writing it in a style that offers the most appropriate perspectives for the Web-based learning audience. It also means selecting graphics, illustrations, and tables that exemplify key points or summarize information in meaningful ways. As with any instruction, involving visual designers in content creation is critical because their input directly affects the content's physical appearance.

● **Determination of subject matter accuracy:** The credibility of a learning intervention is directly proportional to the accuracy of the information it presents. SMEs play a critical role in conceptualizing, shaping, and reviewing the information presented in any electronic learning program. Ensuring the validity of the content that is being developed establishes credibility with learners and helps ensure that the desired training outcomes are achieved.

● **Interaction and interface design:** The visual design of the Web site should be appealing and consistent with good instructional design. A well-designed user interface reduces the need for additional training on how to use the online learning program. It can also increase the accuracy of user responses because they can concentrate on the critical learning task instead of trying to decipher hard-to-read or hard-to-understand directions. The less ambiguous the intent of the functional directions on a Web page, the more likely that users will engage in the activities presented by means of that Web page or screen.

> *Note:* A training manager may need to negotiate compromises between the instructional designers and the visual designers because their goals may conflict in some cases (for example, when innovative and stimulating visual effects detract from the instructional material).

● **Quality control:** Throughout the development phase, ongoing assessments of the quality of the content, navigation, and other aspects of the Web site should be incorporated to identify and correct any problems as early as possible.

● **User testing:** During the development phase, the team will also conduct usability (alpha and beta) tests with members of the target population. This level of testing offers additional opportunities to catch errors and provides valuable data on the materials' ease of use and that of other critical functional components.

● **Technology:** Site development must take into account any constraints imposed by the computer equipment and software in use. In addition, security issues must be resolved prior to development.

- **System operation:** Well-written and well-produced resources cannot have the intended impact if learners have technical difficulties in accessing them. Take steps to ensure that servers are operational, networks are configured appropriately, client or learner machines have the necessary operational capacity and connection capabilities, and appropriate browsers and plug-ins have been installed.

Implementation

In this phase, your WBT program is presented to the learners. During this phase, you will address

- users' expectations

- functionality

- unanticipated effects of the computers, modems, operating systems, browsers, and other software and hardware in use

- any unanticipated effects of programming changes

Scheduling for the initial implementation should include time to find and correct software problems. Incompatible computer configurations, operating systems, and browsers also are likely to cause problems during implementation. If the systems are standardized throughout the organization and the program has been designed on and for those systems, problems should be minimal. But, more often than not, employees in an organization are using a variety of computer platforms, operating systems, and browsers. If they have been told to expect the problems that occur, they are less likely to be frustrated and to discount the entire program. Thus, it is critical that users be warned of potential problems they may encounter and told how they should respond if a problem does occur (for example, call the training and development department, report the problem, and wait to hear from someone there before taking action).

Evaluation

The evaluation phase begins when implementation begins. In this phase, you assess the effectiveness of the training intervention with these questions:

- Are we meeting the objectives that were set in the design phase?

- Are members of the intended audience using the intervention?

- Are there transmission or end-equipment issues that prevent certain trainees from using the system?

- What are the reactions of those who use the training? Do they feel it meets their needs?

- What revisions must be made?

Focus particularly on user feedback and test validity and reliability. It is important to gather information on users' reactions to the online program. The users' initial reactions are likely to affect their use of the learning system. In addition, it is critical that test item analyses be conducted to determine the reliability and validity of any assessment and testing components.

At the end of the implementation, an evaluation of results can serve as a guide for changes and as a justification to upper management for undertaking additional learning experiences. (Sample evaluation instruments are included in chapter 8.) Ask the following questions:

● How did the users rate the program?

● Did the users feel that learning was valuable?

● Can the learners do what the design indicated they would be able to do? Can they apply the knowledge or skills in their work?

● Was it worth it in terms of the perceived benefits (e.g., what the users learned, the potential or real impact on productivity)?

● Would we do it again?

Maintenance

The results of the evaluation phase will point out revisions and modifications that need to be made to the WBT program. Furthermore, technology changes that take place periodically within the organization will require occasional program modifications. Finally, changes in the company's strategic objectives and goals will lead to alterations in training and instructional materials. Remember to advise users when revisions will or have been made (See chapter 8 for greater detail on handling revisions to the instructional and other materials, changes to the visual appearance, and organizational upgrades in technology.)

Need for Ongoing Support

Throughout the entire development process, you will need

● support of key influencers

● committed SMEs

● dedicated personnel from the IT department

In developing an online training program, the support of an organization's key influencers is critical. Key influencers are those people who can allocate the funds needed to develop and implement the program and whose support encourages others to make use of the program. Throughout all phases, the support of key influencers will facilitate the process. As the WBT program manager, one of your primary functions will be to garner the support of key influencers in your organization. Develop a good working relationship with them. You also should foster the commitment of SMEs who can identify which competencies and skills are most important for effective performance and guide the content development.

In general, you will be responsible for obtaining support from the IT department. That support is essential to ensure a successful implementation of a WBT system (in part, to address the technological issues described in chapter 4). Use Checklist 5.1 on page 72 to plan for and track your progress through the six phases of program development.

Additional Considerations

The course designers chosen for the project also will face some specific challenges before beginning the design and development of a Web-based program:

● Web-based courses may not look like previous courses. This is especially true in training and performance support arenas for learners who are working to keep up with rapidly changing developments in their jobs and to advance in their careers.

● Because the tolerance for traditional courseware is decreasing now that learners can access material easily and rapidly in an increasingly "wired" world, the demand for online resources may be high and may lead to tight development schedules.

● The information that is presented must be focused. Because of the ease of access offered via the Web, it is tempting to offer too much information.

● Course design strategies increasingly must account for learner-determined action and yet accommodate instructor-directed and other traditional learning approaches, as appropriate.

● Courses need both to focus on content mastery and to emphasize performance outcomes effectively.

● Course designs must offer worthwhile interactive exercises that address the outcomes expected from an interaction rather than the expected actions of the participants. In other words, the exercises should focus on what the user learns from the interaction rather than on what the user does during the interaction.

Checklist 5.1. Project management checklist and planner.

Phase	Action	Completion Date

Assessment	Identify training needs
	  ● conduct interviews
	  ● review relevant documents
	Identify training solutions
	  ● review existing courseware
	  ● conduct interviews
	  ● evaluate training systems
	Identify technology and software issues
	Complete discovery	

Design	Design instructional resources Design navigation of site Design "look and feel" of site Define reports and statistics desired	

Development	Develop instructional resources
	Program or define navigation of site
	Develop visual design
	Conduct quality assurance
	Conduct user testing
	  ● alpha
	  ● beta
	  ● final
	Program or refine reports and statistics	

Implementation	Develop and distribute materials about the training program Announce date of implementation Introduce users to the site	
Evaluation	Collect user evaluations Determine the validity and reliability of assessment components Analyze user feedback	
Maintenance	Refine/modify site, as appropriate Conduct ongoing evaluations and maintenance	

By accommodating the unique aspects of a WBT program, your training and development group will be able to offer employees these benefits:

- greater access to training resources within the organization

- opportunities to demonstrate initiative, self-direction, and self-motivation

- training and development that is available anytime and anywhere

- all the advantages of distributed learning systems (that is, online training)

▼ ▼ ▼

As a manager, it is critical that you have a solid understanding of each of the phases of WBT design, development, and implementation. Your role in several of the process phases discussed in this chapter will be covered in greater detail in subsequent chapters.

Online Exercise 5. Interaction on the Web.

A: Interacting with Other People

- The purpose of this exercise is to give you an opportunity to experience interaction with others in an online environment. The exercise also gives you a chance to register as a user and complete an optional user profile.

Step 1
Open your browser.

Step 2
Go to: www.yahoo.com

Step 3
Click on the link to: My Yahoo!

Step 4
Register a username. (Remember to record your username and password because you will use them for additional exercises in this book.)

Step 5
Go to one of the message boards (pick something of interest to you). Search a number of boards to find one that is fairly active.

Step 6
Post a message.

Step 7
Review responses to your posting and post additional messages for several days.

Questions
- Was registration easy to accomplish?
- Did you choose to enter optional personal data? Why or why not?
- How long did it take to find an active message board?
- Were you surprised by the nature and tone of messages on the board (for example, did the posted messages follow conventional norms for communication)?
- Did the tone of messages, either yours or others', differ from how you would communicate with someone in person? If you chose not to enter personal information, did the anonymity of your postings cause you to be more direct, blunt, or rude than you might otherwise be?

- If you chose to be more direct or blunt in your postings than you would be in other communications, how did you it make you feel?
- How might the tendency to be more honest and direct using online communication be used to advantage as part of a WBT program? What disadvantages could it present?

  Note: Research into online communication suggests that workers feel more comfortable conveying negative information to their bosses using e-mail than with face-to-face communication.

B: Interacting with Graphic Effects

- This exercise introduces you to some simple graphic effects and gives you an opportunity to select a Web site and manipulate its graphics. The tool you will use is WEBfx. Although many online animations, graphics, and other multimedia require downloading a plug-in, WEBfx is a graphics manipulation tool that you use right over the Web, without downloads, plug-ins, or Java. With WEBfx, you can manipulate any site on the Web by typing in its URL and then choosing the effect you want to create from a pull-down menu.

Step 1
Go to: http://zippy.sonoma.edu/kendrick/webfx/

Step 2
In the center of the WEBfx page you will see a place to enter a URL (http://   ). Type in the URL of a site that has images on it. If your organization has a Web site, enter its URL (for example, www.astd.org). If you get a response indicating that there are no images at the site you've selected, enter another URL until you find one with images.

Step 3
Per the instruction on the WEBfx page, first choose an image and then an effect. Click on the Apply Effect space.

Step 4
Enter other URLs and try different effects.

Questions
- How did it feel to be interacting with your computer screen to create the effects?
- Was the experience more engaging than simply reading text or viewing graphics on the Web?

- Were you frustrated by any aspects of the experience (for example, slow Net response, difficulty finding a URL that worked, or difficulty understanding the instructions)?
- Did the experience change your perception of the value of interactivity when using the Web? If so, how?

If you wish to try out additional interactions with the Net, the same site offers a number of games and other options.

C: Interactivity and Synchronous (Real-Time) Interaction

- The purpose of this exercise is to give you an opportunity to interact with the Web while simultaneously interacting with others. To work this exercise you must have registered with My Yahoo!

Step 1
Go to: www.yahoo.com

Step 2
Click on Yahoo! Games. If you have trouble finding the link, do a search on "Yahoo Games."

Step 3
Choose from among the various games (backgammon, blackjack, euchre, hearts, and so forth).

Step 4
Begin playing a game.

Step 5
While you play, interact with other players by typing comments into the space beneath the game.

Questions
- How did it feel to interact simultaneously with the Web (playing the game) and with the other player(s)?
- Was the experience pleasant, or did you feel overwhelmed by the need to focus on the game and, at the same time, interact with others?
- Did the experience affect your perceptions of interactivity as part of a training program? If so, how?

Chapter 6. The Right Features and Benefits: The Manager's Perspective

As a training manager, one of your primary responsibilities in developing WBT is to establish budget and resource priorities. Most of those critical decisions will be made during the design phase. Budgets for WBT projects vary significantly, depending on the features and benefits desired and on a number of other factors. Practical Tip 6.1 provides a series of questions to help you develop a budget for your particular project.

Some of the key decision issues for selecting the right features and benefits for your WBT will focus on these features:

- Course content and customization

    ○ How will the course content be administered?

    ○ Will prepackaged content be customized, or modified as necessary?

- Job skills and competencies

    ○ What content and resources are needed to meet the specific requirements of each job category, based on the skills and competencies of the job?

- Authoring tools and templates

    ○ Will the development team be using authoring tools or templates to create content?

    ○ What types of templates are available?

- User registration and payment

    ○ How will users register?

    ○ Will users have to pay for any of the courses or resources?

- Site access and security

    ○ How will users gain access to the site?

    ○ How will passwords be created?

    ○ What other security issues have to be addressed or accommodated?

6.1 Budgeting for Web-Based Training

Cost estimates for WBT vary dramatically. Brandon Hall, author of *Web-Based Training Cookbook* (1997), notes that he has heard estimates ranging from $5,000 to $135,000 per finished hour of training. Obviously, the cost will depend on the complexity of the training program and the features and benefits incorporated as well as related technology costs.

You may wish to work with an internal or external consultant who can help you identify the likely costs. The following questions can point out items that should be included in your budget proposal:

● Does the content currently exist in some other format, or will it need to be developed from the beginning? As with any training endeavor, the greater the amount of content development needed, the higher the cost.

● Does your organization currently have the technology and software needed to implement the Web site without additional expenditures? If technology or software is needed, could it be part of the organization's overall IT expenditures, or must it be accounted for as a training expense?

● Is the staff needed to complete the online training program available and in-house? How will their time be billed? Will it be billed explicitly to training?

● Will outside vendors and contractors be needed to accomplish the goals of the project?

● Is adequate time available to complete the project? If not, additional resources may be needed (for example, independent contractors, programmers, outside vendors) and the costs will rise.

● What types of media will be used? Do any of the multimedia components already exist within the organization or must they be developed from the beginning? Multimedia development can be one of the most expensive components of a WBT program.

● What level of interactivity is desired? The greater the interactivity offered, the more complex the site will be and the higher the costs of development and maintenance.

● Will the site include assessment, testing, and certification components? Do these components currently exist for the content that will be used in the site, or must they be developed?

- Course catalogs

  - How will users be made aware of courses and other program offerings?

- Usage statistics and reports

  - How will usage be monitored?

  - What types of reports would be useful for assessing the success of the program?

- User profiles and individualized prescriptions

  - Will the program offer users updated information about their progress?

  - How will the program guide users to make best use of the site?

- Self-assessments

  - Will the site offer an assessment component that guides users to the resources and course offerings that are most appropriate for each of them?

- Testing

  - Will the site offer a way to test what the user learned from a WBT resource?

- Certification

  - Will the site certify employees in organizational products, programs, or other areas of critical importance?

- Personalized professional development plans

  - Will the site include a database that maintains personal data, such as courses and assessments completed, and that summarizes this information as part of an individual development plan?

- User assessment, testing, and certification records

  - What types of records concerning assessment and other testing results will be available?

  - Who will have access to these records?

- Forums (asynchronous) and seminars (synchronous)

  - Will the site offer bulletin boards and other asynchronous communication possibilities?

  - Will the site offer real-time (synchronous) events?

- Practice and reviews

  ○ Should users have access to practice and review materials in addition to other resources?

- Resource libraries and access to online resources

  ○ How will the site link users to resources, both within the site and to external sites?

- Career planning

  ○ Will the site offer information about career planning and development, and if so, what types of information?

- Customization of interface designs

  ○ What degree of customization is needed? (This is especially relevant if you decide to choose a commercial training system.)

Features of Web-Based Training Systems

Each of the features and benefits listed above is described below in greater detail to help you make critical decisions about what to include in your program. You can view some of these features online by working Online Exercise 6.

Course Content and Customization

A number of learning systems offer prepackaged course content that may meet your company's needs. But it is likely that an organization has proprietary information and other specific knowledge and skills that need to be customized to meet training needs. You should determine how the various online systems handle customized content and what support is offered to develop such content. Certain systems allow for very little customization of content and design; others are highly customizable.

Content creation also may involve developing entirely new course materials or modifying existing training materials. In either case, ask these questions about what to place on the Web:

- Is a Web-based approach for these materials likely to be better than a print-based program or a classroom-based course? Why or why not?

- Whom does the audience comprise, and where are they located?

- What reactions might the audience have if a classroom-based course is changed to a Web-based course?

- What has been the reaction to these types of course materials in the past?

Job Skills and Competencies

Performance gaps and training needs are measured by identifying competencies associated with actual job performance. By first defining the necessary competencies for each job, your training and development group can then establish performance objectives to use as standards for comparison with actual performance. Some commercial learning systems offer job skills databases as part of the software package. Most also offer consulting services. How much you want to rely on prepackaged job analyses or consulting is your judgment call based on design, budget, and other considerations.

When designing WBT, determining the gap between the desired and the actual performance is the foundation for a high level of organizational performance success. Identifying those standards is critical for any training effort, including Web-based learning programs.

Authoring Tools and Templates

Most, if not all, Web-based learning systems support one or more authoring tools, such as Macromedia's Authorware and Director, Asymetrix's Tool-Book II, or Allen Communication's Quest. In some cases, the systems offer authoring templates and other tools that negate the need for a separate authoring program, depending on the development team's needs. Answer these questions when choosing or developing a WBT system and the authoring program associated with it:

- In-house expertise with the authoring program

    - Do current staff in the organization have expertise in the authoring program?

    - If so, will those staff members be available for this project?

- Program ease-of-use, especially if in-house expertise is not available

    - How easily can the authoring program be learned?

    - Does the program require considerable expertise to use?

- System programming or hard coding

    - How much flexibility will the final program offer for content revisions, additions, and other modifications?

In general, developers prefer the ability to modify the course content and visual appearance. Hard coding of content and design does reduce flexibility, but often it increases the program's power and stability.

Familiar software packages, such as Microsoft PowerPoint, can offer the design options needed for a training program, especially when the training is being developed with a limited budget. Simple presentations can be placed on the Web, and learners can download the files to their computers. The use of student notes with slides can create effective and relatively inexpensive training resources.

Another important question to ask when making authoring and template decisions concerns how much control an administrator has over modifications to content and visual design. Complicated programming options provide little advantage to nontechnical staff and will add to the ongoing costs of maintaining and refining the site.

User Registration and Payment

When an employee has a profile, the system should enable him or her to register immediately for courses. Some organizations may wish to charge users for taking a course or for using a resource, and several of the commercial training systems support payment through a secure commerce server arrangement.

Site Access and Security

An organization can grant access only to authorized users by distributing passwords or some other sign-on identifier that restricts access. Access to the site can also be limited only to those authorized to enter the company intranet. If you have a secure intranet on which the training Web site can be placed, you may not need to address security issues directly, but make sure that the IT department has those security measures in place. A more significant step is to ensure that all members of the intended training audience have access to the secure site. Training materials or resources that are proprietary make security an extremely important part of your system.

Course Catalogs

One of the most critical components of a WBT program is the information that directs potential users to the training resources. The design and development of the display and listing of courses and other available resources deserve considerable attention. If your training materials are excellent but users don't know they're out there or can't get to them, the program will suffer. In general, the site should have several links to the catalog throughout the system, and have the catalog prominently displayed in the resource library (Figure 6.1).

Usage Statistics and Reports

Monitoring trainee use and providing management with summaries of use by region, job title, and other categories will help the training and development team assess the effectiveness of the site's training and information interventions (Figure 6.2). Most commercially developed systems provide a number of usage reports, and many allow for customization. One training system may meet the organization's needs better than another, depending on the types of reports needed. When evaluating commercial systems or developing a custom program, have your team prioritize the types of reports needed in order of importance.

User Profiles and Individualized Prescriptions

A user profile gives each user a unique identity and tells the training system what training best meets that person's needs. The profile data comprise personal and contact information that allows the system to offer the user WBT in the most personalized way possible. Using information such as the trainee's job title or other job-related information, the training system can direct the user to specifically relevant resources. As a result, the time and energy that each user devotes to training focuses on what is most worthwhile and/or required for that user. For example, sales personnel would select from a listing of available courses or resources different from that of administrative personnel.

Figure 6.1

A sample course catalog screen.

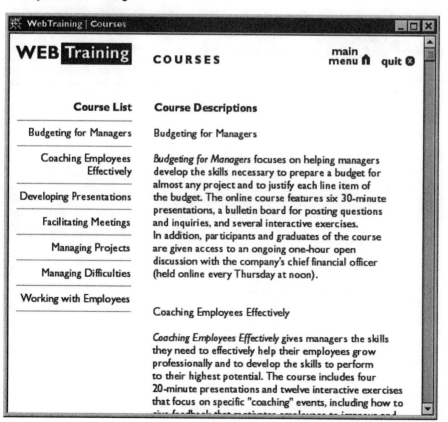

The profile data also enable you to track the progress of specific employee populations (for example, the sales force or the administrative division) in completing professional development and training goals.

Self-Assessments

An assessment function enables trainees to identify competency and development needs in a safe, confidential, and objective environment (Figure 6.3). This function also directs users to appropriate professional development and training resources.

Testing

Most WBT programs place testing activities after the use of training and professional development resources. The tests generally are similar to those administered for any training experience, but on a WBT system, after a user completes a recommended resource (for example, a CD-ROM or online

Figure 6.2

A sample administration screen that includes a user statistics and records component.

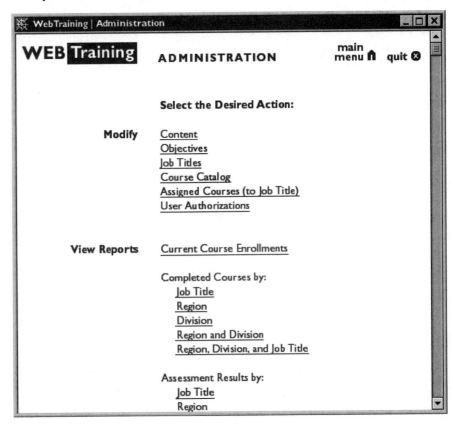

course), the system can automatically test the trainee's mastery of that resource, score the responses, and record the result.

Certification

Your organization may want to certify users' knowledge of key company programs, services, products, and other job competencies. For example, if an organization has a proprietary sales methodology that is critical to its success, the system should be able to test and certify trainees' knowledge of that methodology. Reliable and valid assessment, test, and certification items are important system components, but their design, development, implementation, evaluation, and ongoing maintenance may substantially increase the cost of the WBT program. The value of feedback and of trainees' accountability for learning the materials generally justifies that added cost.

Figure 6.3

An example of a scenario-based question in a self-assessment.

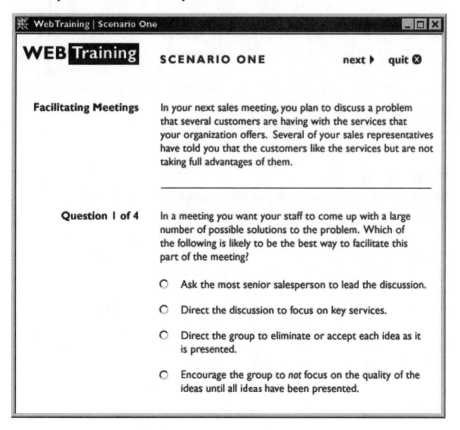

Personalized Professional Development Plans

One of the advantages of WBT is its ability to identify a user's skill and competency gaps quickly. To capitalize on this advantage, customize both the look and content of a personal professional development plan that guides the user to resources including classroom-based training, WBT, online performance support tools, and offline resources such as print materials and CD-ROMs. More sophisticated programs include one or both of the following for each trainee:

● **Personal page:** A personal page maintains a summary of the user's assessment, testing, and certification activities as well as progress toward meeting professional development goals. The progress report can use both graphic and text-based formats. In most cases, the user can navigate to the training and professional development resources and access the complete contents of the resource library from the personal page.

● **Dynamic progress report:** A progress report can be presented in both graphic and textual formats and offers users an up-to-date record of their progress (Figure 6.4). A progress report gives users ongoing reinforcement toward reaching their professional goals and can provide recommendations that facilitate those goals (Figure 6.5, page 88).

User Assessment, Testing, and Certification Records

User assessment, testing, and certification records usually are extensions of the user's personal page or progress report, and including them increases the complexity of the program and thus the cost and the development time. But, as noted earlier, assessment activities are very important components of a WBT program because they give users significant feedback and make them accountable for what they learn.

Forums and Seminars

Interacting with other students and instructors is a critical element of learning environments on the Web. Such interactions may be asynchronous (for example, forums or bulletin boards where users post messages or questions and receive responses at a later time) or synchronous (for example, seminars with live interactions among participants). The offerings may be regularly scheduled events, such as weekly live discussions with instructors, other training personnel, and anyone else who chooses to join in, or may involve real-time chat rooms where individuals can interact with other employees who are online at any given time. The possibilities are unlimited and will depend on the needs of the organization. Such interactions are likely to increase employees' use of and interest in the training site.

Practice and Reviews

In addition to the training and assessment functions, a WBT program can be designed (or customized using several of the commercially available systems) to include practice and review components as part of the learning environment (Figure 6.6, page 89). These can include self-tests, interactive exercises, games, and other practice activities that complement a course or other online training resource. For example, a customer's business problem could be presented, and the learner would indicate the product solutions that would meet that customer's needs most fully. The system would then react to the learner's choices and explain why or why not they were the best choices.

Resource Libraries and Online Access to Resources

A resource library conveys learners to training and instructional resources by including links to those resources (Figure 6.7, page 90). With this function, a

Figure 6.4

An example of a progress report for a manager.

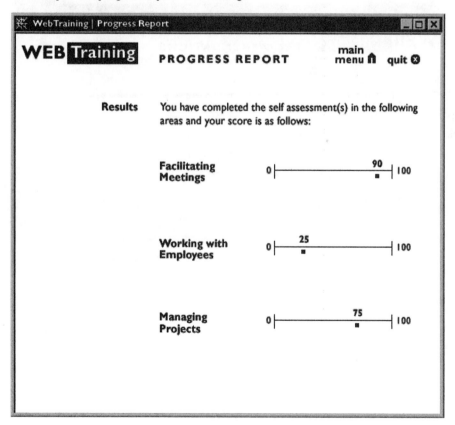

user can reach resources and view, download, or order them, as appropriate. The resource library may also include catalogs with descriptions of the materials and courses the organization offers, and link to other online sources. From the resource library, users can sign up for courses online. Direct access to external online modules and resources may also be offered at this stop on the training site, but check with the IT department to determine how connecting to outside resources affects a user's access to the training site.

Career Planning

You can design the training program to enable employees to see the job requirements and performance expectations for positions that they wish to pursue. Employees wanting to move up in the organization can test their

Figure 6.5

An example of a recommendations screen that shows which resources are recommended on the basis of the trainee's self-assessment results.

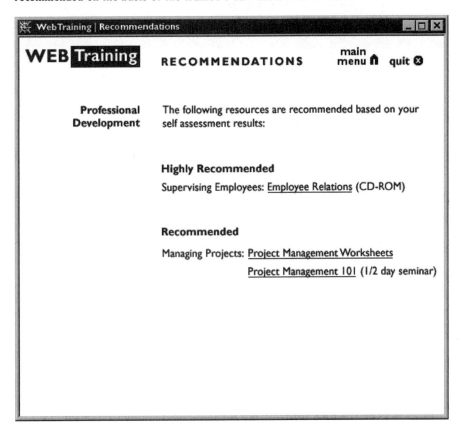

current performance level to gauge how well it compares with the expected performance of the position they wish to move into in the future.

Customization of Interface Designs

The look and feel of the training site can affect its effectiveness a great deal. Most organizations have visual elements (for example, logos and other visual signage) that define their identities (Figure 6.8, page 92). For example, a corporation may use specific colors in all marketing and informative materials. Most likely, the training and development group will want to incorporate your company's visual identity and other look-and-feel components in the training site. By doing so, employees recognize how the site is connected to their corporate identity and sense of purpose. Before choosing a commercial training system, determine how easily it can be customized to incorporate your organization's visual materials.

Figure 6.6

An example of a practice and review screen.

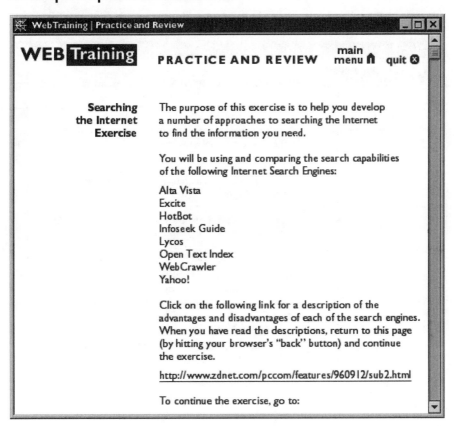

Using a Commercial Training System

Even if you choose to develop a Web site using one of the many commercial training systems vendors rather than producing the complete training package in-house, you will have to consider each of the above features and benefits. Commercial systems often offer basic functionality with add-ons for extra features. By determining which features will contribute to your training program, you can select and pay for only those features that serve the specific needs of your organization. Dozens of vendors offer training systems; here are some of the more well-known ones with their URLs listed for easy access:

- Asymetrix Librarian   www.asymetrix.com

- Digitalthink   www.digitalthink.com

- Learning Tree   www.learningtree.com

Figure 6.7

A sample of the introductory screen to a resource library.

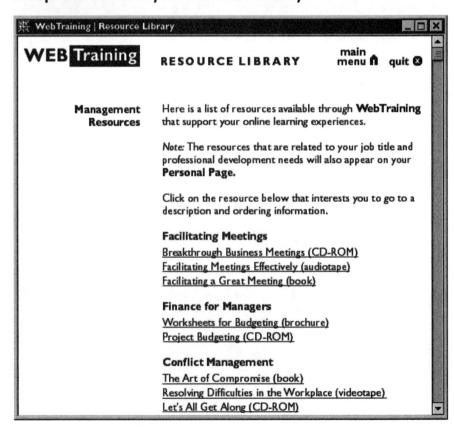

- Lotus LearningSpace   www.lotus.com

- Oracle Training Plan Builder   www.oracle.com.sg/education/

- PrepOnline   www.computerprep.com

- RealEducation   www.realeducation.com

- TopClass   www.wbtsystems.com

- WebLearn Plus   www.informania.com

Each of those training systems offers administrative and management functions that track and measure the use of the learning environment. Using one of the commercial vendors' systems may well meet your organizational training needs. The system's expense will depend on the level of sophistication (that is, the features and benefits) you choose to incorporate.

▼ ▼ ▼

Now that you have an appreciation for a training system's possible components, use Checklist 6.1 to determine how critical each feature or benefit is to your training objectives and to the needs of your organization. Use whatever rating or notation system best meets your needs. Online Exercise 6, on page 94, shows you some of the components in action as parts of commercial training systems.

Figure 6.8

Two examples of the main page of a WBT site.

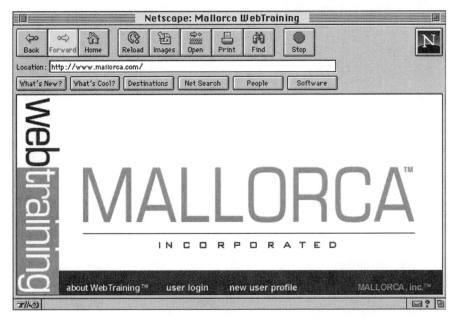

Checklist 6.1. Manager's overview of features and benefits.

Online Components, Features, and Benefits	Significance Rating for Your Organization
● Prepackaged course content	
● Customized content	
● Identification of job skills and competencies	
● Authoring tools and templates	
● User registration and payment	
● Site access and security	
● User profiles	
● Individualized prescriptions based on user profiles	
● Course catalog	
● Usage statistics and reports	
● Assessment	
● Testing	
● Certification	
● Personalized professional development plans: personal pages and progress reports	
● Assessment, testing, and certification records	
● Forums, seminars, and other interactivity components	
● Practices and reviews	
● Resource library and online access to resources	
● Career planning	
● Customized visual design	

Online Exercise 6. WBT program features and benefits.

- This exercise introduces you to the available features and benefits of a WBT program by looking at a number of the commercial training systems.

Step 1
Open your browser.

Step 2
Go to one of the following sites:

For a guided tour of the features and benefits of a training system:
www.asymetrix.com/products/librarian/
- Click on "Take an online tour of Librarian!"
  Click on "Librarian Student Tour."
  Here you will view a sample course catalog and a sample progress report as well as the basic functionality of Librarian.
- Click on "Librarian Administrator Tour."
  Here you will view the tools that the training administrator can use to indicate which courses are associated with which job titles, the types of reports desired, and other administrative features.

  For an overview of how Librarian works, click on the "Asymetrix Librarian Overview."

For a guided tour of an online assessment tool:
www.informania.com/weblearn.html
- Click on the screen, then click on "guided tour." This will give you an experience with scenario-based assessments, including a certification component.
- Return to the Main Menu and click on "simulation."
- Take the simulation. This introduces you to how an online assessment looks and functions, and shows you a sample results page and progress report.

Questions
- Did the guided tours increase your understanding of the features and benefits that a WBT program can offer?
- Were the instructions easy to follow?
- How did you feel about the visual design of the sites?
- Were the guided tours effective as instructional devices?
- What other reactions did you have to these sites and their presentations of features and benefits?

Chapter 7. Constructing the Instructional Web Site: Staffing and Managing

This chapter will identify the functions of all those involved in constructing an effective WBT program, with particular focus on the training manager's role. In general, it is not the training manager's role to know in detail the technical aspects behind construction of the site. That detailed knowledge will come from the experience of the development team that the manager selects (and which can include in-house and external staff, as appropriate). The training manager's primary task is to determine the necessary staff, oversee their activities, and guide them toward meeting the objectives of the site. (See Practical Tip 7.1 for a list of questions that address additional development considerations for training managers.) Once the basic concept and design have been developed and the schedule has been set, the creation

---

Practical Tips

7.1 Additional Development Considerations for Managers

- How much content is needed?
- Is every instructional resource relevant, including links to other resources?
- Does the visual design of the site complement the instructional design and support the training objectives?
- Has a comprehensive approach been developed to ensure the quality of the content and the functionality of the program?
- What expectations have been set regarding the construction of the site?
- Are team members working together in a spirit of cooperation and flexibility?

of the Web site can begin. The design documents developed earlier will guide this process and will help members of the development team understand the objectives and other elements of the entire program.

Staffing Needs

Staffing needs for a WBT project depend on the complexity of the training involved and of the Web site you are creating. A basic development team is likely to include any or all of the following:

- project manager
- instructional designer
- visual and graphic artist
- programmer
- editor/online quality assurance manager
- subject matter expert
- testers (users)
- Web site manager

For Web sites with interactive and multimedia features, including video or audio, the development team also may include the following:

- multimedia programmer
- video scriptwriter
- video production staff

For larger projects, the team may include a second tier of management—individuals serving as lead instructional designer, lead visual or graphic artist, lead video scriptwriter, and so forth. Use Checklist 7.1 to determine your staffing needs.

Staffing Roles and Responsibilities

Project Manager
Primarily, the training project manager oversees the assignment and completion of tasks and outlines the development process and schedule, keeping the entire team up to date on the project's progress, including changes as they occur. Like any effective manager, the project manager needs to be accessible to the team and able to provide necessary resources, encourage-

ment, and support. An effective manager keeps the team focused on the larger picture and working together toward a common goal. The project manager also may serve as an instructional designer or a content editor. Of course, other team members may have overlapping skill areas as well. For a comprehensive list of an effective manager's characteristics, see Practical Tip 7.2.

Checklist 7.1. Staffing needs.

Use the following checklist to determine your staffing needs.

Job Title	Sample Questions	Needed for This Implementation?
● Project manager/ lead	In addition to your role as manager of WBT and development, is a manager or lead also needed? How large will the development team be? Do you need different project leads for subgroups (e.g., visual design lead, instructional design lead)?	❑ Yes ❑ No
● Instructional designer(s)	What types of instructional materials be developed? Will you use prepackaged content? Will you need customized content?	❑ Yes ❑ No
● Visual or graphic artist	What types of screens must be designed? Are you using a commercial training training system that allows for customization?	❑ Yes ❑ No
● Programmer	Are you creating a custom WBT system? What type of database will you use?	❑ Yes ❑ No
● Editor/online quality assurance manager	What types of instructional and design resources will the development team create? What types of programming features will be included in the site? Will the team develop them?	❑ Yes ❑ No

continued on page 98

Checklist 7.1, *continued*

Job Title	Sample Questions	Needed for This Implementation?
● Subject matter expert	What instructional materials and other resources will be developed? Does prepackaged content need to be reviewed for relevance and accuracy?	❑ Yes ❑ No
● Users/testers	How will course content and other instructional resources be assessed prior to deployment?	❑ Yes ❑ No
● Webmaster	Who will maintain the site?	❑ Yes ❑ No
● Multimedia designer	Will the site include multimedia components that must be developed?	❑ Yes ❑ No
● Video scriptwriter	Will the training and instructional materials include video that needs to be developed?	❑ Yes ❑ No
● Video production staff	If video is developed, who will produce the video?	❑ Yes ❑ No

Instructional Designer(s)

Instructional designers develop the content and ensure that the graphics and programming aspects are consistent with the principles of quality instructional design. Although the majority of their writing and other work will occur early in the development process, instructional designers must be available to work with the other team members throughout the project. Instructional design is the heart of any training intervention, and having experienced, talented designers on your team is critical. SMEs can provide content for the training, but it is important to have instructional designers develop that content for any training interventions. Checklist 7.2, on page 100, covers the primary issues that should be addressed by the work of the instructional designers.

Visual and Graphic Artist(s)/Interface Designer

The primary responsibility of the visual and graphic artist is to develop an appealing and user-friendly visual design—that is, a visual design that aids the user's navigation and use of the WBT program. In addition to the graphic aspects of the system, the artist may also create animations and other visual site components. A competent and creative visual designer is critical because the visual appearance of the site will influence users' perceptions of the training. Checklist 7.3, on page 101, offers a description of issues pertinent to visual design and multimedia components.

Programmer(s)

System Programmers

If you have decided to develop a custom training system, one of your challenges will be to build a functional system that integrates your team's instructional and visual designs. The system programmer will need to understand the design and user navigation paths at the level of the operating system both to build the program from a functional perspective and to meet the expectations of the instructional and visual designers.

Instructional Developers/Programmers

These programmers focus on integrating the instructional content into the site at the level of the application. The typical tasks for this group include HTML coding and Java scripting.

Note: Some programmers are skilled as both system programmers and instructional developers.

Practical Tips

7.2 Characteristics of an Effective WBT Project Manager

The effective manager can
● focus the team on the overall objective of creating an effective learning environment
● define tasks and outcomes clearly
● delegate tasks while ensuring the quality of the final product
● oversee each aspect of the project by having a good understanding of the critical components of each function and task, including basic knowledge of the technical aspects
● establish appropriate deadlines and monitor the progress of the project in line with the overall schedule for completion
● finalize design and development decisions
● facilitate and negotiate compromise when differences develop among team members
● respond to unforeseen circumstances in a manner that promotes their resolution and keeps the project on schedule
● garner the support and help of key stakeholders, SMEs, and users throughout the organization

Checklist 7.2. Instructional design.

Use the following checklist to determine how effectively the instructional design meets the needs of the target audience and your organization.

● Target audience	Check that the target audience has been thoroughly analyzed by determining whether each of these factors has been investigated:
	❑ prerequisite knowledge/skill
	❑ size
	❑ geographic location
	❑ motivation
	❑ expectation
	❑ preferred presentation style
	❑ job description
● Performance goals for target audience	Check to see that there is a clear understanding of the following:
	❑ desired performance for target audience
	❑ actual performance of target audience
	❑ performance conditions for target audience
	❑ performance criterion for target audience
● Learning objectives	Check to determine whether or not the learning objectives are derived from the performance goals and that they are
	❑ performance based
	❑ measurable
● Learning interventions	Check to see that the learning intervention maps to the learning objectives and that the selected media for delivery are appropriate to the target audience. Determine whether a rich variety of strategies, including motivational strategies, have been included. In particular, check for opportunities for the target audience to
	❑ practice new behaviors
	❑ get feedback on behavior
	❑ ask questions and get answers
● Assessment and evaluation	❑ Check to see that assessment items meet the criterion for performance and that they have been approved (determined to have face validity) by the SMEs.
	❑ Determine that reviews by SMEs and the target audience have occurred at development milestones and that feedback from those reviews has been incorporated whenever possible.

Checklist 7.3. Interactive (visual and multimedia) design.

Use the following checklist to evaluate the visual components of the site.

● Consistency	Check for consistency among the following visual elements: ❑ typeface ❑ color ❑ spacing/chunking of text groups ❑ typographic hierarchies (headings and subheadings) ❑ placement of buttons and icons ❑ navigation patterns ❑ similar action on buttons (e.g., pop-up windows display charts only) Do the objectives correspond to the specific training needs and solutions that were identified in the design phase?
● Appropriateness	Check the appropriateness of the following visual elements: ❑ aesthetics (the "look") ❑ typeface ❑ color ❑ composition (e.g., background patterns, animations, designs) ❑ text-heavy vs. image-heavy site (e.g., too much text, distracting images) ❑ icons vs. text buttons (i.e., which graphic would most ease navigation for the intended audience?)
● Technical issues	Determine whether each of the following issues has been thought through by the developer(s): ❑ palette compatibility ❑ graphic size and file compression (e.g., JPEG vs. GIF files) ❑ screen resolution output ❑ screen flexibility vs. constrained size ❑ required plug-ins ❑ browser type and version number ❑ platform (e.g., PC or Mac) ❑ distribution (e.g., connection speed, bandwidth, T1, or modem)
● Navigation	Check to ensure that the following navigation issues have been addressed: ❑ real estate size vs. one-click access to information ("Real estate" refers to the size of the Web site.) ❑ orientation identifiers through consistent use of color, text highlights, and rollovers ❑ icons vs. text buttons ❑ pop-up windows ❑ next/back buttons

If you choose a commercial training system, involve your design team in the decision so that they fully understand the features and functioning of the selected system. Otherwise, the team may develop components that are incompatible with the system. Some organizations find that administering and maintaining a commercial learning system and its contents require a permanent, full-time programmer. Checklist 7.4 concerns the major programming tasks.

Database/Systems Analyst

If your training program is to incorporate a database, you will need a database analyst. If there is no database involved, then you will need a systems analyst. The primary responsibility of a database analyst or systems analyst is to work with the team to define what information outputs need to be available. Outputs are presentations of data that can be printed, viewed on the computer screen, or created as files (usually to be passed to another computer). Often, the database or systems analyst develops two specification documents: a functional specification and a technical specification. The functional specifications are for lay readers; they describe functions, but not necessarily the mechanisms that produce those functions. The technical

Checklist 7.4. Programming.

Use the following checklist to determine the level of agreement regarding the programming plan and plans to evaluate the quality of the programming.

● Executability	❑ Check to see whether the programming team has a clear understanding of the functional design and is able to execute it.
● Compatibility	Determine whether the programming team agrees with the interactive design team about the following: ❑ location of any files that are used in a programming task ❑ file-naming standards and version control
● HTML and Java scripting functionality	❑ Ensure that no Java scripting errors occur when a page is brought up. ❑ Ensure that all objects on the page appear (i.e., no broken links, no broken GIF files).
● Quality assurance	❑ Check to determine that QA and the programming team have agreed on the QA plan and procedures.
● Project management	❑ Check to determine that a task list with time assigned to tasks has been created and is being monitored.

specifications, however, must be extremely precise so that the structure, functionality, and relationships among data match the design expectations of the rest of the team. For a smaller WBT project, the database/systems analyst may also be the programmer. (It may help to think of the systems analyst as an architect, and the programmer as a carpenter.) Checklist 7.5 covers database/systems analysis tasks.

Editor/Online Quality Assurance Manager

Even the most carefully designed WBT needs an editor for content review and a reviewer who can ensure the quality and consistency of the site. An online editor does much of what a print-based editor does: he or she ensures that the content is well organized, comprehensible, grammatically correct, and reader friendly, and reviews and suggests modifications to the content developed by the instructional designers.

An online quality assurance manager follows the online course the way an end user would, checking all the functions and features for accuracy, ease of use, and smooth operation, and evaluates the system to ensure that it

Checklist 7.5. Database/systems analysis.

Use the following checklist to determine your technical and functional needs.

● Needs analysis	❑ What data outputs are required? ❑ In what form do the outputs need to be created (print, screen, file)? ❑ What user and systems interfaces are required? ❑ What processes are envisioned to retrieve, store, and manipulate data? (Consider both external and internal processes, i.e., how will data be handled by users as well as the system?)
● Functional specifications	❑ Is the functional specification document comprehensible by lay readers (especially the client and other stakeholders)? ❑ Does the document avoid highly technical or specialized terminology?
● Technical specifications	❑ How is the database laid out (structure, functions, relationships between data)? ❑ What programming language(s) will be used? ❑ What relationships exist among data? ❑ What time-saving steps can be incorporated into the data structure? (For example, a formula to calculate a person's age based on date of birth prevents users from having to type both date of birth and age.) ❑ Are technical specification fully descriptive of data resources, algorithms, and data results?

functions as intended by the instructional designers and visual artists. In some cases, one person may fill the positions of editor and online quality assurance manager, although these roles generally require two specific sets of skills. Checklist 7.6 presents the tasks performed by the online quality assurance manager.

Subject Matter Experts

As noted in chapter 5, SMEs are essential to the development of a WBT system. They serve as the primary knowledge resource and can help define the most appropriate content for the learner population. Furthermore, if the course is going to be marketed, offered to the public, or evaluated by an

---

Checklist 7.6. Quality assurance.

Use the following checklist to assess the quality assurance process.

● Content	Check the quality of the following issues: ❑ Correct spelling, punctuation, grammar, and so forth ❑ Appropriate tone for audience (professional, clerical, or other) ❑ Consistency across writers/developers ❑ "On the Surface" relevance to the needs of the audience
● Visual design	Check the quality of these design issues: ❑ The visual design supports learning. ❑ The visual design is engaging and pleasant. ❑ The visual design is consistent throughout the site (e.g., graphics used for navigation are the same throughout).
● Navigation/ functionality	Check the quality of these navigation and functionality issues: ❑ The program functions as intended (e.g., the system moves the user through the program as designed). Determining that the program functions correctly requires defining *all* the possible paths that a user could take and then testing them. Such testing could be complemented by user testing during the beta phase, but you should not rely on beta testing to ensure that the program functions correctly. ❑ "Unusual" actions do not cause the program to respond incorrectly or to crash. For example, if a user leaves the course in the middle (the user's connection is broken or the user logs out), the program should bring the user back to wherever the developers intended. Testing should include doing everything possible to crash or misdirect the program.
● Cross-platform functionality	❑ If users are on different platforms (e.g., PCs and Macs), test the system with *all* end-user types of equipment, including connection devices (e.g., modems, T1 lines) to ensure functionality and consistency of display across various platforms

outside group, you will need to demonstrate that SMEs were involved in its development, either throughout the project or in certain phases. Get your SMEs in place early in the project. Refer to Practical Tip 7.3 for a list of SME qualifications.

Users as Testers

Although users are unlikely to be formal members of the development team, they are important to the overall development process. Users can participate at various points during development, most notably when user testing is conducted. Testing is commonly done in two phases—alpha, or initial, user testing and beta, or final, user testing of the online system. Testers should be selected from the target audience. Because users who test the course may be doing so in addition to their regular responsibilities and without extra compensation, respect their schedules and demonstrate your appreciation for their help. Practical Tip 7.4, on page 107, describes the two testing phases and how to conduct the tests.

Web Site Manager

In the earlier days of the Internet, one person oversaw all aspects of a Web site. That person was called a "Webmaster." As Web site administration became more complex, one person often could not handle maintaining the functionality, content, visual, interactive, user administration and system aspects of a site. Today, although these responsibilities are often divided among several people, it makes sense to designate one person as the point of contact for the site—the Web site manager. This employee is often part of the IT department or at least maintains connections with that department. The Web site manager may be a team manager or simply may facilitate the

---

Practical Tips

7.3 Qualifications of Your SME

A subject matter expert may be a member of the target audience and should
● be highly regarded by members of the target audience
● be an expert (extremely knowledgeable and experienced) in the topic area
● be strongly committed to the training endeavor
● have a good working relationship with the training staff

maintenance of the site without directly supervising any workers. One primary responsibility of this person is the maintenance of the site as fully functional at all times. This can require a great deal of behind-the-scenes work with technical equipment, servers, and networks. See Checklist 7.7 for a list of Web site manager tasks.

Multimedia Programmer(s)

If you decide to use multimedia in your training Web site (for example, Flash, Director, or other video and audio resources), make sure your developers have a solid understanding of how these media function with various browsers, operating systems, hardware, and software. The multimedia programmers may be the visual and graphic designers as well. If you are not planing extensive use of multimedia, you may choose to hire a consultant to

---

Checklist 7.7. Web site management.

Use the following checklist to determine that all technical and functional aspects of the site are maintained optimally.

● Software and hardware assets	❑ Are software and hardware fully compatible? ❑ Are changes to the site going to affect compatibility? ❑ Is hardware appropriate for site functionality (e.g., is it powerful enough to handle the expected number of users)?
● Full functionality of site, 24 hours a day, seven days a week	❑ Are appropriate resources available? ❑ Is staff readily available to address problems? ❑ Is sufficient power in ready supply? Do the servers for the site need an alternative power supply in case of power loss?
● Iterative development process	❑ As changes are made to the site, is the site retaining flexibility for future changes? Will rewrites be necessary for later versions? ❑ Are specifications for development clear and precise? Are purpose and functionality delineated completely? ❑ Were specifications approved before implementing changes? ❑ Has enough time been allotted to make necessary changes? ❑ Are adequate resources and staff available for development?
● Deployment/ connection with users	❑ Are there conflicts between intranet and Internet protocols? ❑ Is an appropriate server being used? ❑ As user technology changes, what compatibility issues might arise? ❑ Is the site secure (especially important if private, proprietary, or financial information is transmitted)? ❑ If an ISP is used, how does it control security? ❑ How are security and usage monitored? ❑ Do users know how to contact the Web site manager regarding problems they are having?

implement your multimedia functions. Refer to Checklist 7.3 for a slate of multimedia tasks.

Practical Tips

7.4 User Testing, Alpha and Beta

Conducting an alpha test (may involve little or no content)

The primary purpose of an alpha test is to assess users' reactions to
- preliminary visual design
- basic navigational design and functionality
- content topics

Choose two or three typical users from each of your audiences (for example, select by job title or category) to participate in the alpha test. For this test you may bring the users to where the site is being developed or have them access it remotely via the Web.

Review the users' reactions and incorporate them into the ongoing site development. Conduct a structured interview (a predetermined set of questions, similar to those presented in Survey 8.1) with each of the users and record their responses. In general, an interview using open-ended questions is likely to serve you better, but you also may wish to have users complete a written survey such as Survey 8.1.

Conducting a beta test (when the content, visual design, and other site components are completed)

The primary purpose of this test is to assess users' reactions to the completed site, including:
- visual design
- navigation and functionality
- content, including courses and other information resources

Choose four or five typical users from each of your target audiences (this group may include some of the same users who participated in the alpha test, but it should also include people who have never seen the site). For the beta test, the users should access the site just as they will when the site is fully operational (that is, via the Web). Gather the users' responses using the methods described earlier for the alpha test.

Review the users' reactions and make appropriate revisions and modifications prior to implementing the site. If the modifications are significant, you may wish to conduct a second beta test and make a second set of modifications.

Video Scriptwriter and Production Staff

If the site you are designing uses customized video programming, you will need a video scriptwriter. An instructional designer or a full-time in-house scriptwriter may develop the script, or you may hire an external scriptwriter. This member of the team needs some familiarity with the medium of video, because video scripts often require a different approach than do audio or online scripts (for example, they must take into account what visual actions accompany the audio components). Because of the frequent need for special video equipment and studio space, the video component likely will be produced externally (unless your organization has an internal video production staff). Table 7.1 presents the milestones in video production.

Outsourcing

Depending on your organization's staffing situation, each of the tasks described above can be outsourced, including the role of project manager, and often it is easier and more cost efficient to outsource some or all of the

Table 7.1. Video production milestones.

Preproduction milestones	● Production plan developed and approved (including budgets, resource assignments, schedules) ● Scriptwriting: first, second, and final drafts written and approved
Production milestones	● Production resource scheduling including: 　○ on-camera and voice talent 　○ crew and equipment 　○ shooting locations 　○ sound stage 　○ audio recording studio 　○ 2D/3D graphics production 　○ music composition ● Videotaping/filming, audio recording, and graphics production completed ● Additional materials licensed and obtained (e.g., stock footage, stills, music)
Postproduction milestones	● Video edit (rough cut) completed and approved ● Video edit (final cut) completed and approved ● Mastering/video compression/platform testing ● Delivery/duplication (in all required formats, e.g., CD-ROM, compressed files) ● Archiving of all production materials (tapes, storage media) and records (contracts, permission agreements, invoices, talent releases, tracking database)

tasks necessary to develop a WBT program. Organizations such as the American Society for Training & Development, the International Society for Performance Improvement, and the Society for Technical Communications can guide you in choosing an external vendor. If you choose to outsource, make sure that the terms of your arrangement are clear to you and to the external service provider. For example, make sure you understand the extent to which that person or group will be responsible for troubleshooting or for maintenance once they have completed their initial work order. Solicit bids from several service providers before you make your decision.

Development: Making It Happen

Chapter 5 presented the phases of creating Web-based training. When planning for each of the phases, it is helpful for you to create a schedule that clearly delineates individual responsibilities and deadlines. Table 7.2 and Figure 7.1 each present a sample development schedule. The main criterion for judging a timeline's efficacy is each team member's ability to identify his or her responsibilities and due dates at a glance. An effective, realistic schedule will require that team members accept and commit to responsibilities and due dates, so consult them as you create the schedule.

The complexity of your team's involvement and the time they will need to commit will depend heavily on the level of customization involved. Several vendors of commercial training systems offer course content and administration, maintenance and hosting services. If you opt for one of those vendors, the site essentially will be preconstructed. When you use an outside vendor, ask for timeline commitments as you put together your development schedule.

Vision: Keeping the Team Focused

Because technology plays such a crucial role in developing WBT, technological considerations and discussions can overshadow the goals and objectives of the project. The project manager must keep the team focused on the purpose and philosophy of the WBT program. You define the big picture and convey that vision to the team throughout the project. The details of the vision may vary from program to program, but keep the following central aspects of WBT in mind as you describe the macroscopic view.

User-Centered Focus
Everything needs to be learner centered in a Web-based training program because users must regulate and navigate their learning experience.

Table 7.2. Sample WBT project task breakdown and timeline.

Task	Who Completes	Start Date	End Date	Number of Work Days
● Manage the project	project manager	8/1	9/20	(ongoing)
● Research and design tutorial	ID	8/1	8/7	5
● Design user interface	visual	8/1	8/7	5
● Design profile, registration, log-in, evaluation forms	consultant	8/1	8/7	5
● Write design planning document; obtain team and stakeholder approval	team/stake-holders	8/1	8/5	3
● Build technical specifications	systems analyst and programmer	8/4	8/7	4
● Write storyboards (scripts, exercises)	ID	8/8	8/18	7
● Develop screen templates and interface graphics; create the "look"	visual	8/7	8/15	7
● Create audio files	multimedia	8/12	8/21	8
● Develop I-Chat interface/design	programmer	8/13	8/15	3
● Write FAQs, other screen text	ID and editor	8/19	8/21	3
● Implement text, interface changes	team		8/21	
● **All content and functionality locked**		**8/21**		
● Alpha testing (usability testing)	team/end users/internal clients	8/21	8/29	8
● Make changes based on usability feedback	team	9/1	9/5	5
● Beta testing	team/end users	9/8	9/10	3
● Final changes	team		9/14	
● **Deliver final product**	**team**		**9/15**	

Notes: FAQs = frequently asked questions; ID = instructional design.

Figure 7.1. Sample timeline for first 29 days of a WBT project.

Due Date

Team Member	1	4	5	6	7	8	11	12	13	14	15	18	19	20	21	22	25	26	27	28	29
ID	A	A	A	A	A	B	B	B	B	B	B	B			J	J	J				
Visual	C	C	C	C	C	D	D	D	D	D	D	D	D		J	J	J				
Consultant		H	H	H									D								
Multimedia								F	F	F	F	F	F	F	F	F	F				
Systems analyst/ programmer		G	G	G	G					I	I	I			J	J	J				
Project manager	E	E	E	E	E	E									J	J	J				
Users																		J	J	J	J

Tasks Legend:

A = Research and design tutorial

B = Write tutorial scripts and exercises

C = Design user interface

D = Develop screen templates/ interface graphics

E = Write/edit design document

F = Create audio

G = Design forms

H = Design I-Chat

I = Build technical specifications

J = Conduct testing

Content

The content must serve the learner's critical and immediate needs, and any that doesn't should be eliminated. Access to endless resources and information should not be the goal, even if the system permits that easily. Instead, provide access to relevant information that users need to perform their jobs. Throughout the project, work with the SMEs to ensure that the focus of the content is what yields the greatest value to learners.

Visual Design

The primary purpose of the visual design is to support learning. An effective design helps users navigate the site, increases interest in the content, and motivates users to continue to visit the site as a resource. A design that is not supportive of the content—no matter how stunning or innovative—will put the trainee's focus in the wrong place. The design should encourage the learner's engagement with the content, rather than distract from the content.

Technology

The primary purpose of using new technologies is to create more efficient, effective, and flexible learning environments. It may be tempting to incorporate new technologies into the Web site just because you can, but just as with the visual design, using a high-end technological component can distract the user from the content and hinder learning. Be certain you can justify all technological innovations from a learning perspective by asking "How does this benefit the user?"

Expectations of an Iterative Development Process

Developing a successful Web-based learning program is a process of refinement. As training manager, you cannot anticipate every issue that might affect use of the program, including user equipment incompatibilities and programming glitches. Even veteran developers must accommodate changes that become evident and necessary as a site progresses. One of your pivotal management responsibilities is to help the team understand that it must be flexible enough to accommodate changes as they become necessary. And at the start of the project you also may have to elucidate the iterative nature of Web-based development to other members of your organization so that they will be more receptive to the changes or delays that might occur.

▼ ▼ ▼

Now that we have covered in detail the phases of creation for a WBT intervention, including the roles and responsibilities of all members of the training development team, turn to Online Exercise 7 and take a sample course.

Online Exercise 7. Taking an online course.

In this exercise, you will take an online course that teaches you to make simple searches on the Internet. This free course is offered by Digitalthink Corporation. You will have a chance to evaluate this course in Online Exercise 8.

Step 1

Go to www.digitalthink.com/catalog/in/in100/instructor.html

Step 2

Register for the Simple Searching course (this introduces you to a user registration/profile page).

Step 3

Once in your "locker," explore such features as *chat* (synchronous or real-time interaction similar to a forum) and *discuss* (asynchronous interaction similar to a bulletin board).

Step 4

Begin the course, posting to the discussion area when indicated and completing the exercise (this introduces you to online exercises and the use of audio files).

Step 5

Take the quiz and view your results (this introduces you to online testing and display of results).

Questions

- Did you learn something from the course?
- Did you enjoy taking the course?
- Were the instructions, from registration to course completion, easy to follow?
- What aspects of the course did you find particularly effective?
- What aspects of the course did you feel were not effective?

SECTION THREE

Evaluation and Maintenance Issues

Chapter 8. Evaluation and Maintenance of Web-Based Training

When your WBT program has been developed and released, you can expect to make changes, refinements, and upgrades. Even the most meticulously developed programs require modifications. To ease this process, set up a system to collect and analyze data from the users where and when problems occur, and to gather their comments on how to improve the system.

User feedback will come mainly from surveys or questionnaires (see Survey 8.1, beginning on page 118, for a sample instrument). The survey instruments may include items with numbered responses, open-ended questions, or both. Numbered responses enable you to summarize and communicate the results fairly easily because the responses can be averaged and presented numerically in a number of ways (e.g., medians, modes). Open-ended responses, although more difficult to summarize, are likely to capture reactions that may be missed using only a numbered format. For example, an open-ended question such as, "What is your general reaction to the training program?" can provide information that a series of numbered responses might fail to elicit. Surveys that rely exclusively on numbered responses often fail to determine user's reactions to specific design features simply because a comprehensive evaluation of all features would make the survey tedious. An open-ended question that asks what design features the user particularly liked and disliked makes it possible to collect that information without creating a burdensome evaluation instrument.

One advantage of Web-based learning environments is that user evaluations can be administered and compiled by the system. In other words, the system provides users with evaluation instruments at the appropriate times (for example, when they have completed a course), stores the responses, and analyzes and summarizes data from all respondents or from a designated subgroup. A good training system will enable you to compile information about how people in a particular job category or geographic region react to the program. You simply enter your desired "qualifiers" (for example, job category, region, or division), and the system will generate reports of results organized by those qualifiers. With those reports you can assess how the training content and materials are evaluated by members of various

target audiences. Such functionality of a WBT system saves time and effort by eliminating the manual distribution of the surveys and the collecting, compiling, and analyzing of data.

What Should Be Evaluated?

All aspects of your WBT program should be evaluated. Brandon Hall, the author of *Web-Based Training Cookbook* (1997) lists the criteria below for that evaluation:

- **Content:** Does the content meet the needs of the target audiences?

- **Instructional design:** Is the training designed to support learning?

Survey 8.1. Sample online training program evaluation.

Please help us continue to improve the online training resources that are available to you by circling the number that best indicates your level of agreement with each of the following statements and by responding to the open-ended questions.

Key to circled responses:

1 SA	=	I strongly agree with the statement.
2 A	=	I agree with the statement.
3 N	=	I neither agree nor disagree with the statement.
4 D	=	I disagree with the statement.
5 SD	=	I strongly disagree with the statement.
NA	=	Not applicable

1. The online training resources focused on the skills I need to grow professionally.

1	2	3	4	5
SA	A	N	D	SD

2. I liked the visual design of the site (the look and feel).

1	2	3	4	5
SA	A	N	D	SD

a. Which aspects of the visual design did you like?
b. Which aspects of the visual design did you not like?

3. The visual design of the site supports learning (does not distract from the learning aspects of the site).

1	2	3	4	5
SA	A	N	D	SD

- **Interactivity:** Are there interactive components, and do they support learning and effectively engage users?

- **Navigation:** Is navigation through the site simple and consistent?

- **Motivational components:** Are the incentives for using the site effective? Do users perceive that the site will help them grow professionally and be rewarded in the organization?

- **Use of media:** Do the various media used in the site support learning, or do they distract the learner?

- **Evaluation (for example, assessments, testing):** Do users perceive that the evaluation components accurately assess their skills and effectively gauge their reactions to the site?

4. Navigation and instruction throughout the site were simple and easy to follow.

1	2	3	4	5
SA	A	N	D	SD

5. I found the content of the site to be engaging; it held my attention.

1	2	3	4	5
SA	A	N	D	SD

6. The tone of the content was professional.

1	2	3	4	5
SA	A	N	D	SD

7. The online assessments accurately measured my mastery of the material (if applicable).

1	2	3	4	5
SA	A	N	D	SD

8. The site offered the appropriate amount of information.

1	2	3	4	5
SA	A	N	D	SD

9. I enjoyed using this site.

1	2	3	4	5
SA	A	N	D	SD

10. What other reactions did you have to the site?

- **Aesthetics:** Does the visual design support learning or distract from it?

- **Record keeping:** Does the training system store the records that are needed to evaluate a learner's progress as well as overall statistics regarding use of the site?

- **Tone:** Is the tone appropriate and supportive of learning?

Survey 8.2 is based on those criteria, and it asks specific questions that focus on how each criterion can be measured or assessed. For experience evaluating online sites, work Online Exercise 8.

Although online evaluations make it easier to collect user feedback, they also can affect the nature of the responses, especially when users fear repercussions if they evaluate the program negatively or when they believe that positive responses will benefit them somehow. It is possible to create anonymous surveys online, but users must believe that their anonymity is ensured. Many people doubt the security or anonymity of any online transaction. After trainees have used passwords and other identifiers to log on to the course, they are unlikely to believe that the authorship of an evaluation at the end of the course cannot be traced. As a result, if anonymity is essential, it may be necessary to send out printed surveys that can be returned anonymously.

Data Validity and Reliability Issues

Part of the overall success of a WBT program depends on users' perceptions that the system will assess their knowledge accurately. This requires that any assessment items be valid and reliable. Establishing the validity and reliability of test items is absolutely critical if the results of the testing are used to hire, promote, or in any other way affect someone's job status. In such cases, where there are legal requirements and potential legal consequences, a professional statistician should assess the validity and reliability of the items. Valid items test what they are intended to test; that is, if the test is about the ability to facilitate a meeting effectively, valid test items are appropriate measures of that ability.

SMEs often are called in to evaluate whether test items actually measure a trainee's ability to perform or to understand what needs to be done to perform effectively. That type of validity is referred to as "face" validity.

If a test is used to hire, fire, promote, or make other personnel decisions, the items must also have "predictive" validity, which implies that an accurate prediction of subsequent performance can be made on the basis of how well a person does on a test. Predictive validity is more difficult and costly to establish and requires the expertise of a testing professional. To avoid the

Survey 8.2. Manager's evaluation of a WBT program.

To complete this survey, use whatever rating system meets your needs—for example, 1 to 10 or excellent to poor.

Criterion	How Measured	Overall Rating and Comments
● Content: Perceived relevancy and comprehensiveness		
● Instructional design: Does the design facilitate learning?		
● Interactivity: Are users engaged in meaningful ways?		
● Navigation: Is navigation intuitive? Is the site map effective? Do users get stuck? Are navigational icons consistent?		
● Motivational components: Does the site engage users and motivate them to use it?		
● Use of media: Are video, audio, animation, and other visual and audio effects used effectively?		
● Evaluation: Are the assessment, testing, and certification components valid, reliable, and useful?		
● Aesthetics: Is the program visually appealing? Are audio segments pleasant to hear?		
● Record keeping: Do learners feel that the summaries of performance are useful and accurate? Are the records and reports useful to those who access them?		
● Tone: Is the tone perceived as professional?		

legal ramifications of tests used for personnel selection and other decisions, many training organizations opt to have their WBT program's testing function considered an "assessment tool" or some other learner guide.

"Reliability" refers to how well a test provides consistent results over time. If a person takes a test at two different times without an intervening training course and his or her scores are similar each time, the test score can be described as a reliable measure of the person's knowledge. A more detailed discussion of test validity and reliability is beyond the scope of this book, but Checklist 8.1 offers some general testing criteria to help you develop valid and reliable test items that can assess learners' need for or understanding of training materials. For more information on constructing tests, see Westgaard (1993).

Ongoing Maintenance

Every system needs a Web site manager who will keep the site running and answer users' questions. Even if the content and design are excellent, frustrated users will abandon the system if they have difficulties in using the program and cannot find answers for overcoming those difficulties. To respond to standard questions, include a frequently asked questions page with a search function. A user with a query about the site can go to the FAQs page and enter a word or phrase to search for an answer. If the FAQs page does not provide an answer, the user can then e-mail the Web site manager for help. If the question is thought likely to arise again, the Web site manager may wish to add it with a response to the FAQs page.

The site could also include a "suggestions box," where users could place ideas for improving the training program or the Web site. The Webmaster and the training and development group should meet periodically to review the suggestions, decide which suggestions would enhance the site, and then work to incorporate them. (Practical Tip 8.1, on page 124, includes a number of questions that the group should address regarding ongoing maintenance.)

User Administration

Primarily, user administration involves granting or denying access to the training program or to elements of it. A standard component of most online training programs is a system that quickly provides new users with access and denies access to anyone who is either not eligible or has had some change in access rights. This is especially critical when the content of the site includes proprietary or confidential organizational information and materials. Many companies use passwords or employee identification numbers to control access to their internal Web sites. In such cases, the human resources and IT departments generally grant and deny access based on an employee's current job title. When a worker is hired, access is granted; when a worker resigns or is terminated, the rights are eliminated. In some cases, training and development may need to work with IT to grant or to limit access to specific training elements on the basis of job category or some other qualifier.

Checklist 8.1. Constructing valid and reliable tests.

• Face validity: quality of the questions	❑ On the surface (as evaluated by SMEs and others), do the items seem to be reasonable? ❑ Do the items address the content they are intended to address?
• Face validity: quality of the answers	❑ Is the correct answer obvious (i.e., does the correct answer stand out from the other answers)? ❑ Are the correct answers usually the longest answers? ❑ Is the correct answer usually choice "C"? ❑ Are all of the incorrect answers plausible (i.e., are any of them "giveaway" incorrect answers)? *Note:* In general, avoid the use of "All of the above," "None of the above," and "Both A and B"-type responses. Also, four responses is the optimal number.
• Validity: item analysis	❑ Are there any items that the majority of those who do well overall tend to miss consistently? (Indicates there may be a problem with the item.) ❑ Are there any items that those who do poorly overall tend to get correct consistently? (Indicates the item may be too easy.)
• Reliability	❑ Do those who do well on the tests outperform those who do poorly? ❑ Do individuals score roughly the same if they take the test a second time without having had some type of training or other instructional intervention between tests? *Note:* Several sophisticated analyses can be conducted to assess the validity and reliability of items. Depending on how the results of your tests are used (e.g., as a basis for promotions or hiring decisions), you should engage an expert to assess the validity and reliability of the items and overall tests. If hiring and firing decisions are made on the basis of test results, the validity and reliability of the test must be documented or legal action by test takers may be warranted.

Technology Updates

Technology changes at an organization. As the person in charge of WBT, you have to keep informed about such changes. Developing a good relationship with the IT or MIS department is one of the best ways to be in the loop when it comes to knowing about potential and anticipated hardware and software changes. You also need a clear understanding of how technology changes may affect the training Web site and its functioning. If you have any questions about how a change in equipment or software might affect your program, ask someone knowledgeable as soon as possible so that modifications either to plans for technology changes or to the training program, can be made in time to ensure ongoing use of the training site. In some cases, IT and MIS departments will suggest changes solely because the technology is "better," not because it improves the users' use of the technology. As a key representative of those who use the system, your voice is critical.

Ensuring Ongoing Participation

The success of a WBT program will be measured both by its initial impact and by ongoing use of the site. After the training program is introduced, the challenge is to maintain interest in the site and what it offers and to ensure that the training content meets the ongoing and changing needs of the organization. Here are several actions that can be taken to encourage ongoing participation:

● **Changing the visuals seasonally:** Over time, users tire of the same visuals, and that leads to a corresponding decrease in motivation to use the site. Updating the visual design on a regular basis increases users' perceptions that the site is both dynamic and up-to-date, and it raises their motivation to

---

Practical Tips

8.1 Ongoing Maintenance

● How will revisions and updates be handled?
● Who will administer the WBT program and respond to user questions and comments?
● What plans exist to ensure workers' ongoing participation in the WBT program?
● Does the current budget support ongoing maintenance?

access the site even if simply to see what has changed. If the visuals never change, it is harder to see how the content is changing to reflect the evolving needs of the users.

- **Hosting regularly scheduled training and development forums and seminars:** Regularly scheduled forums and seminars that focus on current issues within the organization and meet workers' current needs can be one of the most powerful ways to ensure ongoing participation. If employees know that every Wednesday at noon they can get answers to their most pressing questions, they will be there, especially in larger organizations, where it is difficult to determine which person to call for help with a particular question and even harder to find people at their desks.

- **Requesting and responding to user suggestions on a regular basis:** If users see that their suggestions for improving the site are implemented, their involvement and satisfaction with the site will increase. Fostering a sense of site ownership is one of the best ways to ensure ongoing participation.

- **Informing users of new offerings and programs:** Informing users of new program offerings and improvements in the site serves to remind them of the site and increases the likelihood that they will visit and use it.

- **Updating resources to reflect new company programs and strategic objectives:** To prompt a perception that the site is up-to-date and useful, the site must incorporate new company programs and objectives as soon as is feasible. When a new program is announced, employees have questions and they look for answers. If the training site develops a reputation as one place to find those answers, it will increase employee visits to the site.

Scheduled Revisions

Revisions and other modifications are part of maintaining WBT, but it is critical that revisions be announced in advance. They should also be done on a regular basis (for example, quarterly or semiannually), rather than haphazardly. Significant changes in content or format should be pointed out when announcing the revisions. Practical Tip 8.2 provides a list of steps that are likely to facilitate the process of making revisions. The following example illustrates the impact that unscheduled revisions can have on users.

> Several salespeople at a medium-sized electronics company were discussing the new sales methods as presented in an online course. Two of the salespeople were adamant that it was a four-step methodology. The other three said that it was a five-step process. The group contacted the training and development division to settle the matter. T&D told them that both groups were correct, based on the training

each had received. After three trainee groups had gone through the initial program in which it was described as a four-step process, the SMEs insisted that the training be changed to include a fifth step. T&D could have eliminated the sales staff's confusion (and potential anger) had they informed the first three training groups of the change. Minimally, T&D could have told the newer groups that the process had originally been conceptualized as a four-step process and that some of their colleagues might continue using a four-step approach until they learned about the change.

In that example, if training and development had informed the users in advance of the change, there would have been little or no confusion. As it was, the department's reputation within the organization suffered, and its personnel had to spend time rebuilding its reputation rather than focusing on enhancing its ability to meet the employees' performance support needs.

▼ ▼ ▼

The principal goal of a maintenance program is to refine the site continually so that it meets the changing needs of individual users. The next chapter will address this issue in greater detail.

Practical Tips

8.2 Handling Revisions

The following process will make revisions easier and ensure that users are informed of modifications in content and information.

● **Step 1:** Summarize suggestions, comments, and other reactions received in a weekly or biweekly status report.

● **Step 2:** Meet biweekly or monthly to discuss suggested revisions. Decide which revisions should be made and create a development schedule. The development schedule may include content revisions, visual design changes, new content, navigation changes, and modifications to the assessment components. If necessary, define a budget and set dates for reaching specific milestones.

● **Step 3:** Depending on the extent of the revisions, go through the first three phases of the alpha-to-omega model described in chapter 5 (assessment, design, and development).

● **Step 4:** Implement the changes on a scheduled basis (for example, quarterly) or, if necessary, as soon as required. Be careful to provide uses with ample notice.

Online Exercise 8. Evaluating Web sites.

- The purpose of this exercise is to give you a chance to evaluate several training sites.

  Use a copy of the evaluation in Survey 8.1 and respond to items 2 through 10 to evaluate two or more of the sites listed below. You may also evaluate any sites mentioned in chapter 6 or another site of your choosing.

  www.asymetrix.com/products/librarian/
  www.digitalthink.com/catalog/in/in100/instructor.html
  www.informania.com/weblearn.html
  www.esocrates.com
  www.oracle.com.sg/education/

Chapter 9. Learning and Performance Improvement: Supporting the Individual

One of the greatest benefits of a WBT program is the support it offers individual learners. For example, the ability to access instruction and vast databases of other information resources at the learner's convenience, regardless of time and place, is a benefit that no other medium can match. In addition, a WBT program can assess individuals' current professional development needs and direct them to the resources that best meet their individual professional development needs.

Self-Directed Learning

One of WBT's primary characteristics is its focus on self-directed learning, defined as "a training design in which trainees work at their own pace, without the aid of an instructor, to master predetermined material" (Derryberry and Gomberg, 1998, p. 17). The major strength of such learning is the flexibility it offers both the learner and the training developer. The popularity of self-directed or independent learning results from that flexibility and from its ability to meet diverse training needs within large organizations. Individuals often prefer self-directed learning because they can select learning tasks that they feel they are capable of achieving, that is, for which they have self-efficacy. People generally choose activities at which they believe they can succeed. By allowing them to learn at their own pace, self-directed approaches can help individuals increase their perceptions of self-efficacy and grow both professionally and personally.

Coupled with the Web's ability to offer training anywhere and anytime, self-directed learning takes on an even greater degree of learner independence. At the same time, WBT helps ensure that any self-directed training materials that individuals use are consistent across the organization and are up-to-date. The advantages of self-directed learning are essentially identical to those of WBT. As a result, a WBT program fully supports self-directed

learning. In addition to capitalizing on all the benefits of self-directed learning, a WBT program also can offer synchronous instruction and other interactive learning experiences.

Online Exercise 9 gives you some self-directed experience in reviewing an array of Web-based learning resources.

Integrating Training and Performance Support

Self-directed learning provides a means for integrating training and performance support. As noted in chapter 2, training targets specific knowledge, skills, or competencies, and performance support works to improve performance by taking into account a wider number of factors that influence performance. Training may be just one component of a performance support intervention that can also address such concerns as access to information, work environment, or job aids and tools. WBT, with its focus on self-directed learning, can bridge the gap between training and performance support, so that learning tools are also performance support tools. For example, in a company that sells such networking components as servers and routers, training and performance support might be unified through the use of a configurator tool that helps network providers create viable networking solutions. The tool would help new employees learn about the company's networking products during orientation, and then would act as a continual performance support tool when the employee needed to present networking options to a customer. Another example of the integration of training and performance support is an online training program that acts as a single resource both for the knowledge to perform one's current responsibilities and for career development and expansion of knowledge beyond that presently required. When performance support is integrated into training, learning becomes an experience of empowerment, rather than just information absorption.

Performance Improvement Environments

As a training manager, you may be responsible for both training and performance support. For the reasons discussed above, it can be highly beneficial to integrate those two functions or to bring them together in the same environment. One method of bringing together diverse performance improvement approaches is called a performance improvement environment. A PIE is "a holistic online environment within which individuals can effectively access an organization's information base to meet personal performance support and training needs" (Derryberry and Gomberg, 1998, p. 18).

Clearly, there are many different formats and approaches to online training and performance support. No one approach is best for everyone or every organization. In small organizations, a PIE may simply be a Web site with links to relevant Internet sites and internal databases. In larger organizations, a PIE may be a highly dynamic environment with a vast range of content and learning mechanisms categorized by user profile (for example, user's job, area of expertise, or level of experience).

A PIE permits a learner to use training and performance support offerings on the basis of individual need. As defined by Derryberry and Gomberg (1998), an effective PIE is

- user centered

- performance focused

- content-neutral

- learning model/design/style–neutral

- delivered by intra-/extra-/Internet

- capable of sophisticated monitoring and management

User-Centered, User-Driven PIE

A PIE supports and is tailored to the needs of the user. This requires matching users' need with content. The mapping of needs to content occurs through the use of information channels—something akin to road maps—that begin with a user's needs and lead to the content that satisfies those needs. Information channels rely on an effective information retrieval system that can couple preferences with information requests in order to customize content.

Performance-Focused PIE

All components of a PIE should be developed with the sole purpose of enhancing performance. A PIE needs to accommodate three distinct elements of performance-related content: task-oriented information, skills- (or knowledge-) oriented information, and competency-oriented information. Each of those elements may require a different perspective and format. For example, task-oriented delivery of information provides the user only with what is needed to complete a particular task (not the "big picture"). Meanwhile, skills-oriented or competency-oriented information may need to be packaged and presented in a more instructional format, with opportunities for practice and feedback.

Content-Neutral PIE

Because WBT courses and internal intranets usually connect to or contain content from a variety of sources or vendors, it is necessary for a PIE to be content-neutral. The structure of the PIE should allow for users to pull con-

tent from a range of sources in various forms without interruption to their learning experience.

Learning Model/Design/Style–Neutral PIE

There are many theoretical approaches to performance support. To accommodate this variety, a PIE has to support all theoretical paradigms for structuring learning. Likewise, because training and performance support programs can be created with endless design and style variations, a PIE must be able to support diverse presentation designs and styles.

Intra-/Extra-/Internet-Delivered PIE

An effective PIE makes use of both company intranets and the Internet. Company intranets usually contain information not available to the public, and the Internet yields access to resources too vast to house on an intranet. Because a learner may need to access content from both sources, the PIE must provide a means to interface swiftly between the two.

Monitoring and Management Capabilities of PIE

An effective PIE can easily be monitored and managed in response to user needs, content changes, and business needs. As user needs change over time, the PIE must evolve as well. Monitoring usage is important because it allows you to delete content that is not used and to develop or expand content that is in high demand. Monitoring also will help you draw connections between the usage of the PIE and business results. Because the Web makes it easier to maintain and refine the PIE, training offered via the Web can fully support the individual needs of the learner.

Summary and a Final Checklist

The success or failure of your WBT program will ultimately be measured by the degree to which it supports the needs of the individual learners whose professional development and growth, in turn, determine the success of an organization. Checklist 9.1 helps you evaluate how effectively your Web-based effort meets individual training needs. You can also use the checklist to identify areas in which your program can be refined to meet those needs more fully. Use the second column in the checklist to indicate how well you believe your program meets the objective or to identify how you might meet the objective more successfully.

Perhaps you and your team should discuss the items in this Checklist 9.1, using the data collected during the site development, implementation, and evaluation. Like all training programs, interventions delivered via the Web are never finished. They must respond over time to changing organizational and individual professional development needs. Nonetheless, successfully implementing a WBT program is an accomplishment to be celebrated. Such a program forms the foundation of a training and development approach that can meet the specific professional development needs of each person in your organization in ways that were not possible only a few years ago.

Checklist 9.1. Does your WBT program meet an individual learner's needs?

Use this list to rate your program for each of the following learner percep-
tions. Note any comments, as appropriate.

User Perceptions	Rating/Comments
● Training program helps them improve professionally.	
● Users have access to information when and where they need it.	
● The amount of material available to users is sufficient, without being so vast that pertinent information is difficult to find.	
● Online support is available to users, and responses are provided in a timely manner.	
● The site offers interactive opportunities that engage users.	
● Users are regularly surveyed to determine what refinements, additional offerings, and updates would address their current needs.	
● Navigation and use of the site is simple and logical.	
● The site's self-assessments and other testing components direct users accurately to the resources they need.	
● Users use the site.	

Online Exercise 9. A self-directed search of learning sites.

● Now you can review an array of WBT sites at your own pace. If you have ever entered the word "training" into a Web search engine, you probably received thousands of "hits." To help narrow your search and to find sites that are particularly relevant, consider beginning your search at one of the following sites:

www.trainingsupersite.com
www.astd.org

The trainingsupersite.com Web site offers links to more than 250 training-related Web addresses and includes rankings of the sites by topic. Those sites can give you all kinds of help as you move forward with your company's WBT initiatives.

Note: There are no questions for this exercise other than the ones you develop and seek answers for using the above Web resources.

Glossary

The following glossary defines many of the important technical terms that a manager of Web-based training is likely to encounter during the various phases of a WBT project. A number of the definitions were standardized in the November 1997 issue of *Training & Development* magazine and later in *ASTD Models for Learning Technologies: Roles, Competencies, and Outputs,* by George M. Piskurich and Ethan S. Sander (1998). The standardized terms are indicated with an asterisk. In addition, several of the definitions are identical to those provided in the ASTD publication *A Trainer's Guide to Web-Based Instruction: Getting Started on Intranet- and Internet-Based Training,* by Jay Alden (1997).

Asynchronous: Communication between two or more people over an extended period of time. Messages are stored so that they can be retrieved at a later date. Bulletin boards and forums are examples of asynchronous communication methods.

ATM: Abbreviation for *Asynchronous Transfer Mode.* ATM is a high-bandwidth (high-speed) alternative to Ethernet. ATM transmission is essentially continuous, and it is an ideal network for multimedia delivery.

Audioconferencing: A form of teleconferencing that allows several people to communicate with each other in real-time (synchronously).

Audiographics: A form of audioconferencing that involves the simultaneous transmission of telephone and computer (voice and image) signals.

Bandwidth: The capacity of a telecommunications channel and how much voice, video, and other data can be handled at one time. Also referred to as connection speed (for example, 14.4 kbps modem, T1 line).

Browsers: Software applications that allow Web users to view and navigate through the Internet (for example, Netscape, Internet Explorer).

Bulletin Board: An asynchronous message board where users can view, post, and retrieve messages from others.

*Cable TV: The transmission of television signals via cable technology.

*CD-ROM (or Digital Video Display): Abbreviation for compact disc-read only memory. A format and system for recording, storing, and retrieving electronic information on a compact disc that is read using an optical drive.

CGI: Abbreviation for *Common Gateway Interface.* A script for processing data written in a Unix-based programming language called *Perl.* It allows a

system (database) to maintain data that is completed by users online (for example, forms, surveys, and other documents), and it stores the data on the Web site's server.

Chat Mode: The sending and receiving of text or voice messages among users in real time (synchronous communication).

Client: Computer system software that occupies a point (or node) on a network and provides functions for users.

Client-Server Architecture: Architecture that distributes the processing load between a client computer and a server computer. Applications (programs) are broken up so that different components run on different computers, thus distributing the load and resulting in more efficient and quicker processing.

Compressed Video: Video images in which the data required for storage and transmission have been reduced using a compression technique (for example, GIFs and JPEGs). Compressed video allows for images to be sent via the public telephone network.

Computer-Assisted (or Computer-Based) Instruction: A form of CBT (computer-based training) in which instructional materials are presented using computer technology. Can be designed to allow learners to proceed at their own pace and to include student interaction.

Computer-Based Training (CBT): A general term used to describe any learning event that uses computers as the primary distribution method; primarily used to refer to text-based, computer-delivered training.

Computer-Mediated Communication: A form of CBT that enables communications between or among people.

Computer (Web) Conferencing: A form of CBT using computer software that enables people to post or respond to messages on pre-arranged topics and subtopics.

Desktop Video System: A videoconferencing system in which audio and video images are transferred to the user's desktop computers.

Digital: Information represented in binary form via a series of discrete, electronic "zero" and "one" bits that are grouped to represent numbers, letters, or images.

Distance Learning: A system that connects learners to educational resources, regardless of time and place.

*Distribution Methods: Means through which information is delivered to learners. Such methods include satellite and cable TV; LAN/WAN networks; computer discs; the Web (the Internet, intranets, and extranets); CD-ROMs; e-mail and voice mail; simulators; audiotapes and videotapes; and telephone.

Domain Name: The written address of a Web site (for example, astd.org or microsoft.com).

Download: The process by which files are transferred from a server to a client.

*Electronic Mail (E-mail): The exchange of messages through computers.

*Electronic Performance Support Systems (EPSS): An integrated computer application that uses any combination of expert systems, hypertext, embedded animation, or hypermedia to help a user perform a task in real time quickly and with minimal support from other people.

*Electronic Text: The dissemination of text via electronic means.

*Ethernet: A LAN-enabling technology that is relatively inexpensive and easy to implement. In this type of network, files are broken into small "packets" of data. The files are "reassembled" at the receiving end, and any missing packets are sent again. As a result, transmissions are reliable but often at the expense of speed.

*Extranet: A collaborative network that uses Internet technology to link organizations with their suppliers, customers, or other organizations that share common goals or information.

FAQs: Abbreviation for *Frequently Asked Questions.* Often listed as part of a Web page to answer common questions asked by users.

File Transfer Protocol (FTP): A coding/programming technique that allows Internet users to send and retrieve files from a server.

Firewall: A security system that limits access to a protected network to authorized users. Allows users within the protected network access to resources outside the firewall.

Frames: The division of a Web page into sections, each with its own hypertext reference.

Full-Motion Video: A video transmission format that provides high picture quality comparable to commercial television.

GIF: Abbreviation for *Graphic Interchange Format.* A compression technique used to save simple graphics.

Gopher: A system that allows Internet users to gain access to and view text-based information stored in a particular format.

Graphic Designer: A person skilled in creating and developing graphic images.

*Groupware: An integrated computer application that supports collaborative efforts through the sharing of calendars for project management and scheduling, collective document preparation, e-mail handling, shared database access, electronic meetings, and other activities.

Home Page: The initial page of a Web site. This page typically presents an overview or table of contents of the site and incorporates multimedia images.

HTML: Abbreviation for *Hypertext Markup Language.* The language used to define the appearance of text and images on a computer screen. The standardization of the language allows all computer systems connected to the Internet to display roughly the same screens, regardless of their operating systems.

HTTP: Abbreviation for *Hypertext Transport Protocol.* The Internet protocol that allows Web browsers to retrieve information from servers.

Hyperlink: An element of a Web page that, when clicked, brings a different part of the page or an entirely different page to the computer screen.

Image Map: A Web page graphic that has separate, active hyperlinks in different parts of the graphic image.

Instructional Design: A systematic process for assessing instructional needs and goals, defining instructional objectives, selecting instructional methods and media, developing materials to accomplish the objectives, and implementing and assessing the training.

*Instructional Methods: Ways in which information is taught to learners. Such approaches include lectures, literature, games, demonstrations, expert panels, case studies, exercises, group discussion, simulations, and role play.

Instructional Strategy: A plan of instructional activities, methods, and media to achieve instructional goals.

Interactive Form: A Web page whose entries (boxes in which the user can insert text, boxes with pull-down menus of selections, and selectable buttons) can be submitted to a server for processing.

*Interactive TV: One-way video combined with two-way audio or another electronic response system.

*Internet: A worldwide network of communication lines that now connects millions of computer users in many kinds of organizations.

Internet Protocol (IP) Address: A lengthy numerical address of a system on the Internet.

Internet Relay Chat (IRC): An Internet resource that enables users to communicate with each other in real-time over the network.

*Intranet: A general term describing any network contained within an organization; used to refer primarily to networks that use Internet technology.

ISDN: Abbreviation for *Integrated Services Digital Network.* A digital telecommunications channel that integrates voice, data, and video and is faster than regular telephone transmissions.

ISP: Abbreviation for *Internet Service Provider.*

Java: A standardized, cross-platform, programming language for dynamically creating and processing data "objects" (applets) on the Web.

JPEG: Abbreviation for *Joint Photographic Expert Group.* A compression technique used to store and interpret complex graphics.

*Learning Technologies: The use of electronic technologies to deliver information and facilitate the development of skills and knowledge.

Listserv: An electronic mailing list maintained by a specialized software program. It allows subscribers to send messages to a large group of people all at once.

*Local-Area Network (LAN): A network of computers sharing the resources of a single processor or server within a relatively small geographic area.

Modem: A communications device for (1) modulation (converting a digital electronic signal to an analog signal so that it can be carried over the telephone), and (2) demodulation (converting the analog signal at the receiving end back to a digital format so that the receiving computer can process the signal).

MUD, MOO, MAUD: Respectively, abbreviations for *Multi-User Domain, MUD Object Oriented,* and *Multi-Academic User Domain.* Internet-based conferencing techniques that provide many users with a common space in which they can communicate and interact with a simulated environment.

*Multimedia: A computer application that uses any combination of text, graphics, audio, animation, and full-motion video. Interactive multimedia enables the user to control various aspects of the training such as the sequence of content.

One-Way Video/Two-Way Audio: The transmission of both video and audio signals in one direction (generally, from an instructor's site to one or more remote sites) with voice-only transmission in the other direction (usually by telephone).

*Online Help: A computer application that provides online assistance to employees.

Palette Shift: Distortion that results from differences in the way a file allocates space for colors. For example, most GIF files allocate space for only 256 colors, but other formats allow for the use of more colors. If used together in an animation sequence, the two palettes will not be compatible and likely will cause some image distortion.

PDF: Abbreviation for *Portable Document Format.* A standardized format for transferring whole pages and documents from one computer to another. Unlike HTML, the pages are transferred intact, like photographs, so that they look identical regardless of the browser that is in use (that is, the appearance of the pages is browser independent). In order to view a PDF document, the browser uses a plug-in called Adobe Acrobat Reader (the plug-in can be downloaded for free from Adobe Corporation at www.adobe.com).

Plug-In: A small software program that allows users to run certain types of multimedia formats on their desktop machines. Generally used to run audio and video programs over the Internet.

*Presentation Methods: The ways in which information is presented to learners. Such methods include electronic text, computer-based training, interactive TV, multimedia, teleconferencing, online help, groupware, virtual reality, audio, video, and electronic performance support systems.

Private Network: A telecommunications network reserved for private use by a single organization.

Protocol: A term used in telecommunications to identify a particular method for accessing data over a network (for example, FTP, HTTP, TCP, IP).

*Satellite TV: The transmission of television signals via satellite.

Server: Computer system software used for storage and processing; it provides all computers on a network with access to common information and resources.

*Simulator (or Tactile Gear): A device or system that replicates or imitates a real device or system.

Streaming Audio or Video: A transmission process by which sound and motion image files are sent to a client system in an active serial form that allows the audio or video to be presented as soon as it is received without waiting for the entire file to be downloaded.

Synchronous: Communication between two or more people that occurs in real time.

TCP: Abbreviation for *Transmission Control Protocol.* Network software that controls the transmission of data over the Internet and is required for computers to communicate with Web servers.

*Teleconferencing: The instantaneous exchange of audio, video, or text between two or more individuals or groups at two or more locations.

Telnet: A telecommunications systems that allows network users to log in or connect to a remote host server in order to access information stored there or to use its software.

Thread: A group of associated postings to a Web conference composed of messages and replies to messages that all relate to a single discussion topic.

Trunk Line (T1): A point-to-point communications circuit provided by long distance carriers for voice and data transmission. In the United States, a T1 transmits at 1.544 megabytes per second (mbps). In Europe, a T1 is known as an E1 and has a speed of 2.054 mbps.

URL: Abbreviation for *Uniform Resource Locator.* A string of characters that supplies the Internet address of a resource on the Web along with the protocol by which the resource is accessed (for example, http).

*Video: One-way delivery of live or recorded full-motion pictures.

Videoconferencing: A form of teleconferencing using compressed video technology to transmit two-way video images and sound between two or more sites.

Virtual Campus: A software application that gives students access to an integrated set of interactive capabilities useful for conducting a course or program of instruction, such as mailing lists, Web conferencing, and synchronous chat.

Virtual Classroom: A real-time software application that mimics instructor and student processes found in typical classroom environments, including the presentation of information, the asking of questions, and the process of feedback.

*Virtual Reality (or 3D Modeling): A computer application that provides an interactive, immersive, and three-dimensional learning experience through fully functional, realistic models.

*Voice Mail: An automated, electronic telephone answering system.

VRML: Abbreviation for *Virtual Reality Modeling Language.* A language used to define spaces (or *worlds*) on the Web, which are composed of dynamic 3D graphics.

Webmaster: An individual with primary responsibility for maintaining and overseeing a Web site and the Web server.

Whiteboard: A software application that allows multiple users to enter content (text, graphics, or other markings) into a common page or document.

*Wide-Area Network (WAN): A network of computers sharing the resources of one or more processors or servers over a relatively large geographic area.

*World Wide Web (the Web): All the resources and users on the Internet using the Hypertext Transport Protocol (HTTP), a set of rules for exchanging files (see HTTP above).

References

Alden, J. (1998). *A Trainer's Guide to Web-Based Instruction: Getting Started on Intranet and Internet-Based Training.* Alexandria, VA: American Society for Training & Development.

American Psychological Association. (1993). *Learner-Centered Psychological Principles.* Washington, DC: Author.

Baron, R.A., and D. Byrne. (1994). *Social Psychology: Understanding Human Interaction.* Needham Heights, MA: Allyn & Bacon.

Bassi, L., and M.E. Van Buren. (1998). "The 1998 ASTD State of the Industry Report." *Training & Development, 52*(1), 22–43.

Blair, D.V., and D.J. Price. (1998). "Persistence: A Key Factor in Human Performance at Work." *Performance Improvement, 37*(1), 27–31.

Derryberry, A. (1998). "Making the Business Case: Predicting ROI for Performance Improvement Environments and Electronic Learning. In *Learning Without Limits: Leveraging the Power of Electronic Learning* (volume 2, pp. 35–48). San Francisco: Informania.

Derryberry, A., and E. Gomberg. (1998). "Performance Improvement Environments." In *Learning Without Limits: Leveraging the Power of Electronic Learning* (volume 2, pp. 17–24). San Francisco: Informania.

"Doing Business in the Internet Age: The Information Technology Annual Report." (1998). *Business Week,* 22 June.

Filipczak, B. (1996). "Training on Intranets: The Hope and the Hype." *Training, 33*(9), 24–32.

Fister, S. (1998). "Web-Based Training on a Shoestring." *Training, 35*(12), 42–47.

Hall, B. (1997). *Web-Based Training Cookbook.* New York: John Wiley & Sons.

Kanfer, R. (1993). "Work Motivation: New Directions in Theory and Research." In *International Review of Industrial and Organizational Psychology* (volume 7), C.L. Cooper and I.T. Robertson, editors. New York: John Wiley & Sons.

Laughlin, P.R., and A.L. Ellis. (1986). "Demonstrability and Social Combination Processes on Mathematical Intellective Tasks." *Journal of Experimental Social Psychology, 22,* 177–189.

Locke, E.A., and G.P. Latham. (1990). *A Theory of Goal-Setting and Task Performance*. Englewood Cliffs, NJ: Prentice Hall.

Masie, E. (1998). "Emerging Acronyms Spell Market Change." *Computer Reseller News,* 27 April.

McCombs, B.L. (1992). *Learner-Centered Psychological Principles: Guidelines for School Redesign and Reform*. Washington, DC: American Psychological Association and Mid-Continent Regional Education Laboratory.

McCombs, B.L., King, J.V., and Wagner, E.D. (1993). *. . . And Learning For All Resource Directory: Model Programs and Practices Transforming Education*. Boulder, CO: Western Interstate Commission for Higher Education.

Miceli, M.P., and M.C. Lane. (1991). "Antecedents of Pay Satisfaction: A Review and Extension." In *Research in Personnel and Human Resources Management* (volume 9, pp. 235–309), K. Rowland and O.R. Ferris, editors. Greenwich, CT: JAI Press.

Ormrod, J.E. (1995). *Human Learning*. Englewood Cliffs, NJ: Merrill/Prentice Hall.

Piskurich, G.M., and E.S. Sanders. (1998). *ASTD Models for Learning Technologies: Roles, Competencies, and Outputs*. Alexandria, VA: American Society for Training & Development.

Pitkow, J.E., and M.M. Recker. (1996). "Results from the First World-Wide Web User Survey." Atlanta: Georgia Tech University. http://www.gvy.gatech.edu//user_surveys/survey-01-1994/survey-paper.html.

Steers, R.M., and L.W. Porter, editors. (1989). *Motivation and Work Behavior* (5th edition). New York: McGraw-Hill.

Wagner, E.D. (1994). "In Support of a Functional Definition of Interaction." *American Journal of Distance Education, 8*(2), 6–29.

Wagner, E.D. (1997). "Interactivity: From Agents to Outcomes." In *New Directions for Teaching and Learning at a Distance: What It Takes to Effectively Design, Deliver, and Evaluate Programs* (pp. 19–26), T.E. Cyrs, editor. San Francisco: Jossey-Bass.

Wagner, E.D. (1998). "Interaction Online: Designing for Outcomes." In *Learning Without Limits: 5 Articles That Unlock the Power of the Web for Training and Development* (volume 1, pp. 11–12). San Francisco: Informania.

Wagner, E.D., and B.L. McCombs. (March-April 1995). "Learner-Centered Psychological Principles in Practice: Designs for Distance Education." *Educational Technology, 35*(2), 32–35.

"Wake Up! (And Reclaim Instructional Design)." (1998). *Training, 35*(9), 36–42.

Westgaard, O. (1993). *Good Fair Tests: Test Design and Implementation*. Amherst, MA: HRD Press.

Resources

The following resources can help you further your understanding of Web-based training and provide you with information and tools to effectively manage a WBT program. The section is divided into the following categories:

- training organizations and professional journals
- WBT vendors (selected list)
- WBT development and delivery tools
- Web resources: organizations, discussion forums, listservs
- selected bibliography

Training Organizations and Professional Journals

The following organizations provide professional publications and other resources to help you manage WBT projects.

American Educational Research Association (AERA), 1230 17th Street NW, Washington, DC 20036-3078. Phone 202.223.9485; fax 202.775.1824; http://aera.net
   Mission: to improve "the educational process by encouraging scholarly inquiry related to education and by promoting the dissemination and practical application of research results."
   Publication: the quarterly journal *American Educational Research Journal.*

American Society for Training & Development (ASTD), 1640 King Street, Box 1443, Alexandria, VA 22313-2043. Phone 703.683.8100; fax 703.683.8103; www.astd.org
   Mission: to "provide leadership to individuals, organizations, and society to achieve work-related competence, performance, and fulfillment."
   Publication: *Training & Development* magazine.

Association for Educational Communications and Technology (AECT), 1025 Vermont Avenue NW, Suite 820, Washington, DC 20005. Phone 202.347.7834; fax 202.347.7839; www.aect.org

Mission: to offer "leadership in educational communications and technology by linking professionals with a common interest in the use of educational technology and its application to the learning process."

Publication: the quarterly journal *Educational Technology Research and Development.*

EDUCAUSE (formed by the merger of EDUCOM and CAUSE), 1112 16th Street NW, Suite 600, Washington, DC 20036. Phone 202.872.4200; fax 202.872.4318; www.educom.edu

Mission: "to help shape and enable transformational change in higher education through the introduction, use, and management of information resources and technologies in teaching, learning, scholarship, research, and institutional management."

Publications: *CAUSE/EFFECT, Educom Review, EDUCAUSE Online, Washington Update, Edupage, EDUCAUSE Professional Papers* (formerly *CAUSE Professional Papers*), and *Proceedings of the EDUCAUSE Annual Conference.*

Information Technology Training Association, Inc. (ITTA), 8400 North MoPac Expressway, Suite 201, Austin, TX 78759. Phone 512.502.9300; fax 512.502.9308; www.itta.org

Mission: to "shape and support Information Technology Education for the future." It is the trade association for professionals and companies involved in the IT Training Industry.

Publication: *ITTA*link *Newsletter.*

International Society for Performance Improvement (ISPI), 1300 L Street NW, Suite 1250, Washington, DC 20005. Phone 202.408.7969; fax 202.408.7972; www.ispi.org

ISPI is the "leading association dedicated to increasing productivity in the workplace through the application of performance and instructional technologies."

Publication: the monthly journal *Performance Improvement.*

Society for Applied Learning Technology (SALT), 50 Culpeper Street, Warrenton, VA 20186. Phone 540.347.0055; fax 540.349.3169; www.salt.org

SALT provides support to professionals whose work requires knowledge and communication in the field of instructional technology. SALT offers individuals knowledge enhancement and improved job performance through society-sponsored meetings and publications. Members gain knowledge in the field of applied learning technology by associating with other professionals in conferences sponsored by the society.

Publications: *Journal of Interactive Instruction Development, Journal of Educational Technology Systems, Journal of Medical Education Technologies, Journal of Instruction Delivery Systems,* and *SALT Newsletter.*

Society for Technical Communication (STC), 901 North Stuart Street, Suite 904, Arlington, VA 22203-1854. Phone 703.522.4114; fax 703.522.2075; www.stc.org

STC is "an individual membership organization dedicated to advancing the arts and sciences of technical communication. Its 22,000 members include technical writers, editors, graphic designers, multimedia artists, Web and Intranet page information designers, translators and others whose work involves making technical information understandable and available to those who need it."

Publications: *Intercom* and *Technical Communication.*

United States Distance Learning Association (USDLA), 2995 Taylor Lane, Suite 4, Byron, CA 94514. Phone 925.516.7377; www.udsla.org

Purpose: "to promote the development and application of distance learning for education and training. The constituents we serve include K through 12 education, higher education, continuing education, corporate training, and military and government training."

Publication: *ED, Education at a Distance.*

***The American Journal of Distance Education,* published by the American Center for the Study of Distance Education, Pennsylvania State University, 110 Rackley Building, University Park, PA 16802-3202.**

WBT Vendors (Selected List)

Digitalthink, 415.437.2800
www.digitalthink.com

Delivers training via the Web to companies and individuals. Courses cover computer science, multimedia tools, the Internet, and other topics.

Informania, phone 415.626.7343
www.informania.com

A performance-improvement consulting firm that specializes in developing technology-based learning solutions.

Learning Tree, phone 800.843.8733
www.learningtree.com
Offers IT training and certification. Delivers training through a variety of media.

Lotus LearningSpace, phone 617.577.8500
www.lotus.com
A combination of software and services for the creation and delivery of online training and education.

RealEducation, phone 303.873.7400
www.realeducation.com
Provides online education services, including development, management, and marketing of courses and degree programs via the Internet.

Socrates, phone 717.523.0030
www.esocrates.com
Offers Web-based knowledge management systems for online learning, education, and training.

WBT Development and Delivery Tools (Selected List)

Authorware 5 Attain (Macromedia), phone 800.457.1774
www.macromedia.com
A visual rich-media authoring tool for creating Web and online learning applications; it allows training developers, instructional designers, and SMEs to develop trackable learning applications and deploy them across the Web, LANs, and CD-ROM.

Designer's Edge (Allen Communication), phone 800.325.7850
www.allencomm.com
A set of integrated pre-authoring tools and wizards to walk trainers through the entire instructional design process, from analysis to evaluation; courses can be exported to other authoring tools for final development or can go directly to HTML/Java templates for online delivery using Net Synergy.

IconAuthor Net Edition (Asymetrix Corp.), phone 800.448.6543
www.asymetrix.com
Icon-based solution for multimedia and Internet-based training; multi-platform program for creating robust interactive learning applications for CD-ROM, network, and Internet delivery; IconAuthor separates application content from logic.

Librarian (Asymetrix Corp.), phone 800.448.6543
www.asymetrix.com

A learning management system for centrally controlling all your learning activities, including course delivery, learner access, collaboration, and performance tracking.

Pathware 3 (Macromedia), phone 800.457.1774
www.macromedia.com

A complete computer-managed instruction (CMI) system for enterprise learning management; Pathware helps instructional designers, content developers, and training managers through every step of the online learning process, from assembling, assigning, and delivering curricula to tracking, storing, and reporting student progress.

PrepOnline (ComputerPREP), phone 800.228.1027
www.computerprep.com

A knowledge-management solution that relies on Internet technology to develop, deploy, and manage online learning and assessment.

QuestNet+ (Allen Communication), phone 800.325.7850
www.allencomm.com

A visual authoring environment for developing interactive training for delivery via CD-ROM, Internet, intranet or LAN, or a hybrid mix of delivery vehicles; uses the Internet for both peer-to-peer communication and client server communication and offers administrator and student management capabilities.

Toolbook II Instructor 6.0 (Asymetrix Corp.), phone 800.448.6543
www.asymetrix.com

A Microsoft Windows-based authoring product that enables authors to create highly customized courseware; offers an array of tools and predefined content (including wizards, templates, and catalogs of pre-scripted objects).

TopClass (WBT Systems), phone 415.392.7951
www.wbtsystems.com

A comprehensive training management solution for a variety of learning applications; the TopClass product family spans all aspects of training management, from assembling courses and tests to moderating collaboration and monitoring results.

Web Learn Plus (Informania), phone 415.626.7343
www.informania.com

Provides a flexible performance improvement environment; offers enterprise-wide learning resource management, access to any content of any for-

mat from any vendor, individualized learning and professional development plans, competency assessment and certification tools, and personal development progress tracking.

Web Resources: Information, Discussion Forums, and ListServs

These Web sites and Web-based resources offer WBT information.

Information Resources

The MASIE Center
http://www.masie.com/
An international thinktank dedicated to exploring the intersection of learning and technology.

Training and Development Community Center
http://www.tcm.com/trdev/
A gateway to a number of WBT sites

Training Supersite
www.trainingsupersite.com
A broad collection of human performance and productivity resources.

WBT Information Center
http://www.filename.com/wbt/index.htm
A nonprofit resource for those interested in developing and delivering WBT, online learning, or distance education.

Discussion Forums

Training Supersite Discussion Board
http://www.trainingsupersite.com/tss_link/disboardset.htm

Web-Based Training Information Center Open Forum
http://www3.web2010.com/filename/forums/open/index.html

ListServs

Association for Educational Communication and Technology
listserv@wvnvm.wvnet.edu
To subscribe, send an e-mail message stating "subscribe aect-I."

Internet Trainers Nettrain List
listserv@ubvm.ca.buffalo.edu
To subscribe, send an e-mail stating "subscribe nettrain [your name]."

DEOS-L Listserv focuses on training from a distance. To subscribe, type <LISTSERV@LISTS.PSU.EDU> in the "TO" line. Type <.> in the "SUBJECT" line. Type <subscribe DEOS-L Your Name> in the "MESSAGE" area. Send.

NETTRAIN is for trainers who teach Internet and Internet-related courses. To subscribe, type <LISTSERV@UBVM.cc.buffalo.edu> in the "TO" line of your Internet e-mail program. Type <SUBSCRIBE NETTRAIN Your Name> in the "MESSAGE" area. Send.

Peer-Assisted Learning Listserv. To subscribe: type <Subscribe PAL> in the "MESSAGE" area of your e-mail program and send to maiser@psychology.dundee.ac.uk.

TRDEV-L Listserv covers a broad scope of training issues, from needs analysis to performance consulting to evaluation. To subscribe, type <LISTSERV@LISTS.PSU.EDU> in the "TO" line of your Internet e-mail program. Type <.> in the "SUBJECT" line. Type <subscribe TRDEV-L Your Name> in the "MESSAGE" area. Send.

WBTOLL-L Discussion List is a discussion area for developers, training managers, educators, students, and others using (or considering) online media in the delivery of training and learning programs. To subscribe, send an e-mail message to listserv@hermes.circ.gwu.edu with the command: sub WBTOLL-L Firstname Lastname. In the body of the message, type your name in place of "Firstname Lastname."

WebTraining-L at Brandon Hall Resources is a weekly forum for technology-based training questions and answers. To subscribe, send an e-mail to WEBTRAINING-L@brandon-hall.com.

Selected Bibliography

Books

Web-Based Training and Instruction

Alden, J. (1998). *A Trainer's Guide to Web-Based Instruction: Getting Started on Intranet and Internet-Based Training.* Alexandria, VA: American Society for Training & Development.

Brooks, D.W. (1997). *Web Teaching: A Guide to Designing Interactive Teaching for the World Wide Web: Innovations in Science, Education, and Technology.* New York: Plenum Press.

Driscoll, M. (1998). *Web-Based Training: Using Technology to Design Adult Learning Experiences.* San Francisco: Jossey-Bass.

Hall, B. (1997). *Web-Based Training Cookbook.* New York: John Wiley & Sons.

Harrison, N. (1998). *How to Design Self-Directed and Distance Learning: A Guide to Instructional Design for Creators of Web-Based Training, Computer-Based Training and Self Study Materials.* New York: McGraw-Hill.

Informania. *Learning Without Limits: Leveraging the Power of Electronic Learning, Volume Two.* (1998). San Francisco: Author.

Khan, B.H., editor. (1997). *Web-Based Instruction.* Englewood Cliffs, NJ: Educational Technology Publications.

McCormack, C., and D. Jones. (1997). *Building a Web-Based Education System.* New York: John Wiley & Sons.

Porter, L.R. (1997). *Creating the Virtual Classroom: Distance Learning with the Internet.* New York: John Wiley & Sons.

Instructional Design and Technology

Cahoon, B., editor. (Summer 1998). "Adult Learning and the Internet." *New Directions for Adult and Continuing Education* (number 78). San Francisco: Jossey-Bass.

Dempsey, J.V., and G.C. Sales, editors. (1993). *Interactive Instruction and Feedback.* Englewood Cliffs, NJ: Educational Technology Publications.

Harasim, L., S.R. Hiltz, L. Teles, and M. Turoff, editors. (1995). *Learning Networks: A Field Guide to Teaching and Learning Online.* Cambridge, MA: MIT Press.

Seels, B.B., and R.C. Richey, editors. (1994). *Instructional Technology: The Definition and Domains of the Field.* Washington DC: Association for Educational Communications and Technology.

Distance Education

Dillon, C.L., and R. Cintrón. (Fall 1997). *Building a Working Policy for Distance Education.* New Directions for Community Colleges (number 99). San Francisco: Jossey-Bass.

Rossman, M.H., and M.E. Rossman. (Fall 1995). *Facilitating Distance Education.* New Directions for Adult and Continuing Education (number 67). San Francisco: Jossey-Bass.

Web Design and Authoring

Dinucci, D., M. Giudice, and L. Stiles. (1998). *Elements of Web Design: The Designer's Guide to a New Medium.* Berkeley, CA: Peachpit Press.

Kristof, R., and A. Satran. (1995). *Interactivity by design: Creating & Communicating with New Media.* Indianapolis, IN: Hayden Books.

Lopuck, L. (1996). *Designing Multimedia: A Visual Guide to Multimedia and Online Graphic Design.* Berkeley, CA: Peachpit Press.

Mok, C. (1996). *Designing Business: Multiple Media, Multiple Disciplines.* New York: Macmillan.

Mok, C. (1996). *Graphis New Media Annual.* Lakewood, NJ: Watson-Guptill.

Norman, D. (1994). *Things That Make Us Smart: Defending Human Attributes in the Age of the Machine.* Reading, MA: Addison Wesley Longman.

Rosenfeld, L., and P. Morville. (1998). *Information Architecture for the World Wide Web.* Cambridge, MA: O'Reilly & Associates.

Sano, D. (1996). *Designing Large-Scale Websites: A Visual Methodology.* New York: John Wiley & Sons.

Siegel, D. (1997). *Creating Killer Web Sites* (2d edition). Indianapolis, IN: Hayden Books.

Siegel, D. (1997). *Secrets of Successful Web Sites: Project Management on the World Wide Web.* Indianapolis, IN: Hayden Books.

Tufte, E.R. (1990). *Envisioning Information.* Cheshire, CT: Graphics Press.

Tufte, E.R. (1992). *The Visual Display of Quantitative Information.* Cheshire, CT: Graphics Press.

Tufte, E.R. (1997). *Visual Explanations: Images and Quantities, Evidence and Narrative.* Cheshire, CT: Graphics Press.

Weinman, L. (1996). *Deconstructing Web Graphics.* Indianapolis, IN: New Riders Publishing.

Weinman, L. (1996). *Designing Web Graphics: How to Prepare Images and Media for the Web.* Indianapolis, IN: New Riders Publishing.

Wurman, R.S., and P. Bradford, editors. (1996). *Information Architects.* Cheshire, CT: Graphics Press.

Return-on-Investment

Phillips, J.J. (1991). *Handbook of Training Evaluation and Measurement Methods* (2d edition). Houston: Gulf.

Articles

WBT and Instruction

Bauer, A.M. (1998). "World wide weeds." Special report: Online learning. *Training, 35*(2), OL6–OL12.

Gordon, J. (1997). "Infonuggets: The bite-sized future of corporate training?" *Training, 34*(7), 26–33.

Maddux, C.D., and D.L. Johnson. (1997). "The World Wide Web: History, cultural context, and a manual for developers of educational information-based Web sites." *Educational Technology, 37*(5), 5–12.

Wagner, E.D. (in press). "Beyond distance education: Distributed learning systems." In *Handbook of Human Performance Technology* (2d edition), H. Stolovich and E. Keeps, editors. San Francisco: Jossey-Bass.

Instructional Design

Pisik, G.B. (1997). "Is this course instructionally sound? A guide to evaluating online training courses." *Educational Technology, 37*(4) 50–59.

Piskurich, G., editor. (1993). "Self-directed learning." In *The ASTD Handbook of Instructional Technology* (pp. 22.1–22.27). New York: McGraw-Hill.

Thiagarajan, S. (1993). "Just-in-Time Instructional Design: How to Do IT Faster and Better." In *The ASTD Handbook of Instructional Technology* (pp. 20.1–20.4), G.M. Piskurich, editor. New York: McGraw-Hill.

Williams, M.D. (1996). "Learner-Control and Instructional Technologies." In *Educational Communications and Technology* (pp. 957–983), D.H. Jonassen, editor. New York: Simon & Schuster/Macmillan.

Performance Support

Grice, R.A. (1989). "Online information: What do people want? What do people need?" In *The Society of Text: Hypertext, Hypermedia, and the Social Construction of Information* (pp. 3–21), E. Barrett, editor. Cambridge, MA: MIT Press.

Reynolds, A. (1993). "Expert systems." In *The ASTD Handbook of Instructional Technology* (pp. 9.1–9.32), G.M. Piskurich, editor. New York: McGraw-Hill.

Web Design and Authoring

Phillips, V. (1998). "Selecting an online authoring system." *Training, 35*(4), 53–61.

Return-on-Investment

Dahl, H.L., Jr. (1987). "Return on Investment." In *Training and Development Handbook* (3d edition). New York: McGraw-Hill.

Hawkins, C.H., K.L. Gustafson, and T. Nielsen. (1998). "Return on Investment (ROI) for Electronic Performance Support Systems: A Web-Based System." *Educational Technology, 38*(4), 15–21.

"How to Conduct a Cost-Benefit Analysis." (1990, July). *Info-Line* (report 007). Alexandria, VA: American Society for Training & Development.

Kearsley, G. (1993). "Costs and Benefits of Technology-Based Instruction." In *The ASTD Handbook of Instructional Technology* (pp. 16.1–16.19), G.M. Piskurich, editor. New York: McGraw-Hill.

Lyau, N.-M., and D.J. Pucel. (1995). "Economic return on training investment at the organizational level." *Performance Improvement Quarterly, 8*(3), 68–79.

Phillips, J.J. (1998). "The ROI Process: Issues and Trends." *Educational Technology, 38*(4), 7–14.

Wagner, E.D., and A. Derryberry. "Return on Investment (ROI) in Action: Techniques for 'Selling' Interactive Technologies." *Educational Technology, 38*(4), 22–27.

About the Authors

Alan L. Ellis is a senior consultant with Informania, an international performance improvement consulting firm based in San Francisco. At Informania, he designs and develops training and professional assessment resources, many of which are delivered via the Web. He has worked with many *Fortune* 500 companies, including Kaiser Permanente, Wells Fargo, Novell, and 3Com. Ellis holds a Ph.D. in psychology from the University of Illinois at Urbana/Champaign, and is the coauthor of several books, including *A Manager's Guide to Sexual Orientation in the Workplace* and *Sexual Identity on the Job: Issues and Services.* He is the author of numerous articles on work-related psychological issues and has presented sessions on Web-based training and small group behavior at ISPI and APA professional conferences. In addition to his work at Informania, Ellis teaches courses in social psychology, social conflict and conflict resolution, and small group behavior at San Francisco State University.

▼ ▼ ▼

Ellen D. Wagner is vice president, consulting services, for Informania. She supervises the design and development services featured in all of Informania's customized performance system implementations and directs the company's assessment, testing, and evaluation operations. Before joining Informania, Wagner served as chair of the educational technology department and director of the Western Institute for Distance Learning at the University of Northern Colorado. She is a former project director with the Western Cooperative for Educational Telecommunications of the Western Interstate Commission for Higher Education. She holds a Ph.D. in educational psychology from the University of Colorado–Boulder and B.A. and M.S. degrees from the University of Wisconsin–Madison.

▼ ▼ ▼

Warren R. Longmire is an instructional designer at Informania, where he develops customized training and performance programs. His background is in both education and training, and he has taught in Japan and Lithuania and at the University of Massachusetts, Amherst. While working in human resources, he developed and implemented orientation and training programs

in educational and financial environments. Longmire also has worked on several editorial projects and assisted in editing Oscar Wilde's plays for Oxford English Texts. He holds an M.A. in English from the University of Chicago, and is currently completing his Ph.D. in English at the University of Massachusetts, Amherst.